Roberto Tirado's Weatherbook

Everybody talks about the weather, but nobody does anything about it.

Anon.

Roberto Tirado's Weatherbook

by Roberto Tirado

 PEREGRINE PRESS, Publishers

Old Saybrook, Connecticut

Cover design by Jill Callaway

Book design by Hildebrandt Associates

Animal prints from *Woodcuts by Thomas Bewick and His School,* edited by Blanche Cirker, 1962, New York, Dover Publications, Inc.

Manufactured in the United States of America

First Printing

ISBN 0-933614-12-8

Table of Contents

Preface

The creation of a book is a joyful, painful task that is almost impossible to describe. I wanted to write a book about the weather that treated the subject with a wide degree of artistic license plus some warmth and humor not usually found in books on meteorology and history. The subject absolutely fascinates me, but I must admit that it sometimes can be fairly dry. Let us hope that is not the case here and that this book will be informative as well as fun.

I must thank numerous people who, in one way or another, helped me with this project. First of all, my thanks go to the wonderful people at the Sterling Library at Yale and the American Meteorological Society in Boston for their gracious help and for making excellent resources available to me. For the same reasons, I thank my good friends at the Wallingford Public Library (despite the fact they always seem to want my money). My sincere gratitude must go to my wife, Linda, who bore the brunt of this madness with the quiet elegance so typical of her, and to my parents, who sent me to college when all we could afford was Twinkies and grape soda. Grateful appreciation must go to George Thompson, a consummate newsman, who not only changed my name to "Roberto," but insisted (against all odds) that I be made a member of this modern lunacy we call "a News Team." Finally, I must admit that none of this could have been done without the cajoling, faith, advice, and patience of my editor, Michael Alan Fox, and my publishers, Barry and Susan Hildebrandt.

Roberto Tirado

How Weathermen Happen

Maybe you've heard the story of the young boy who constantly fibs to his mother about every little thing; finally, one day, mama tells him that if he doesn't shape up and stop lying he will grow up to be a weatherman.

An unfair rap! Like most other weathermen, I lie only for very brief periods on a regular daily schedule—in my case, at 6 PM and 11 PM. And I prefer to call it forecasting.

Although I could make up some pretty good—sometimes even convincing—stories when I was a kid, mostly to explain my whereabouts to my mother, I preferred to think of them as exercises in creative imagination rather than as lying. So it wasn't that character trait that prepared me to be a weatherman, and I never played with old brass barometers or watched weathervanes. I liked playing with cap pistols and haunting Brooklyn movie houses to watch Errol Flynn protect civilization from savages.

Oddly enough, though, it was a lie that started me on the road toward the six o'clock news and high-pressure areas, but by that time I was a scheming adult rather than an imaginative kid. It was a cloudy day in May—looking back at it, I'd say about a 30% chance of showers—when I stumbled over the steps of a local television station in New Haven, Connecticut. I proceeded upstairs to an office marked Public Affairs, absently wondering whether I might have a public affair with some vision of loveliness whose youth and beauty were wasting away behind the door. Had wasted, it turns out: the creature behind the door was not the stuff of which fantasy is made.

"Are you the new researcher?"

"Yes, the gentleman downstairs told me that my services could begin immediately."

So there you have the Big Lie, and I guess it was good enough for the situation. Given the fact that a story on public housing had to be prepared within the next few hours for afternoon shooting, the issue of my qualifications was not raised, and there was no further discussion.

"Here, take this script down to the director and bring it back as quickly as possible with any corrections he makes."

And off I went. I had unexpectedly landed a job in television as a researcher, and this was to save me from having to be a school teacher for the rest of my life. Not that being a school teacher wasn't satisfying: I also enjoy root canal work. But life as an inner-city teacher is depressing when you have some loud-mouthed students who shouldn't be in school at all, and some administrative heads who should be selling cars. Add to this the fact that teachers, after six years of college, earn a fraction of what a New York weatherman makes for telling you that it will be partly cloudy tomorrow.

The director grabs the script from my hand, takes me over to the set, and tells me to keep the questions strictly within the scope of public housing and not to venture out into other areas of inquiry. Does he mean that I am going to host this program? Precisely, just so. With the sweat pouring from my hands and my eyes wide, I watched the red light on the camera go on, and the floor director signaled for me to begin. There is an old Russian proverb that says: "If you go to church, pray once. If you go to war, pray twice. But if you get married, pray three times." To which I can only add that if you are going to host a television program, pray four times.

It is as artificial a situation as you can imagine. You ask penetrating or predictable questions in front of a gum-chewing cameraman and a floor director who flashes you funny hand signals every three or four minutes. It's enough to make anyone a basket case. I fell back on my theatre experience and pretended that I was acting the part of a dynamic, interested host in a play. This immediately implies certain vocal inflections and physical postures: you lean in toward the victim to extract answers to your eloquently phrased questions. The effect can be pretty convincing unless you lean in too close and scare the hell out of your guest. Actually, Steve Allen, himself one of television's great wits, said it best: a television host should be a little dull and not very talented. Which explains Ed Sullivan.

At any rate, I hosted 35 public affairs shows. I didn't make any money at it, because community service and minority-oriented programs are television's stepchildren, with budgets to match. They wouldn't exist at all if the F.C.C. didn't insist on them as a condition for holding and renewing a broadcast license. But they don't make money, so producers are given a budget the size of a teenager's allowance to do them. No glitter, no flash, dreary consequences. You know old people want to laugh and sing and make love and have a hell of a good time just like any of us, but instead of a full-scale production with a chorus of oldsters racing across your screen singing "There'll Be Some Changes Made," what you get is two or three people sitting around on threadbare chairs talking about impending death.

Now, it goes without saying that the boss didn't want me doing anything but minority programs. He reminded me of an old army cook who must have had his taste buds shot off in some war so that everything tasted the same. For him, everyone had to look the same. Credibility is an important quality in television; for him, only people who looked like the Good Humor Man could possess it. Here we are, a hundred different cultures living under one roof, and you need a Good Humor Man to tell you what went on in Washington today? That was television just a few years ago, and when I tried to get on the air five years ago it was as if I had dropped in from outer space. Some Spanish kid telling New Englanders that it will be partly sunny tomorrow? He was sure they would never buy it, and in thousands of New England households there would be constant muttering: "It just ain't right, I tell you, it just ain't right."

Fortunately, with the help of George Thompson, a man of insight and vision, I got on the air. I started as a part-time weather person for a few years before being called to New York to do the weather full-time for WPIX on Channel 11. I am also employed by a top-rated New York radio station, and so I suppose I have made up for the fact that I didn't play with barometers as a kid.

The weather is an important segment of any television news program, so the producers make sure that the weatherman appears almost last on the show. This is known as the "hook" section of the program, since all of you watching want to know if you have to cover your tomatoes tonight. The expectation is that you will watch the entire program to find out if you can wear a light dress tomorrow or if you should be prepared for any eventuality with the layered look. This assures the program's ratings and therefore the station's profits. Important stuff, so ratings are the basis for any decision, and things are not left to chance. They are the reason why the anchorman is cute and well-spoken, the anchorwoman is sexy in a very classy way, and the sports guy is lively with a little suggestion of rippling muscles under the blue shirt. As for the weatherman, well, he gets to be anything he wants to be, except dull. In order to be a good weatherman you must know where all the states are, even though around here you don't find yourself talking very much about Arkansas, where apparently not much distinctive weather happens. You should also know that all weather in the northern hemisphere travels from west to east. This is important, and probably has some influence on us. Maybe if it were the other way around we would all speak backwards and instead of saying "Geritol" we would say "Lotireg" and communications would suffer. Of course, a Hebrew scholar would argue that reading a book from back to front is more interesting, but we can't let that distract us from our main point: our weather comes from California, not Portugal.

The weatherman in the Northeast gets to have more fun than his colleagues in other areas. After a brief rundown of the Big Picture (it's raining in the Pacific Northwest and there's a stalled high in the Southwest—phrases that could almost be permanently written on the weather map), he gets to talk about the most interesting and variable weather in the country.

No one has ever described it better than Mark Twain, who after his idyllic youth on the river boats of the Mississippi, settled in Hartford at the age of 35 to become a Yankee. He hadn't lived there for more than six years when he made his famous weather speech to the New England Society, which remains the definitive statement on the subject: "In the spring I have counted one hundred and thirty-six different kinds of weather within four-and-twenty hours . . . . Probable northeast to southwest winds, varying to the southward and westward and eastward, and points between, high and low barometer swapping around from place to place; probable areas of rain, snow, hail, and drought, succeeded or preceded by earthquakes, with thunder and lightning. . . . Yes, one of the brightest gems in the New England weather is the dazzling uncertainty of it. There is only one thing certain about it: you are certain there is going to plenty of it. . . ."

And of course it has always been that way.

Five Centuries of Weather Disasters

This section will be an attempt to describe, chronologically, all the important weather-related events that have occurred on the Eastern Seaboard since Columbus. They are sometimes terrible, sometimes funny, but each of them had some impact on our history.

Which reminds me: it seems a shame in our technological society that those greatest of all storms, the hurricanes, are given trivial names like Camille or Gladys or David. (To the Camilles and Davids—and whatever more than one Gladys may be—of the world, no offense meant. I think your names are just fine for people. Not so hot for hurricanes.) I much prefer the characterizations given in the early days: *John Winthrop's Sudden Gust* (1643), *the Dreadful Hurry Cane* (1667), *A Great Rain and a Horrible Wind* (1727), the *Windy Week* (1812), and so on; but I have to admit that a storm named Donna has to have more personality than, say, Storm No. 12, which illustrates the prosaic naming scheme used during the 1930s. Personally, I'd just as soon go through life having as little as possible to do with hurricanes. But if it came to that, I think I might be happier to know that my property was totally destroyed by a *Dreadful Havock* (1682); rather than a storm named Bruce.

The Puritans and the Weather

Before we go on to chronicle all of the things that can go wrong and therefore, in accordance with Murphy's Law, have gone wrong with New England weather, it may be helpful to reflect for a few minutes on the Puritan view of the world. If, like me, you grew up in happy-go-lucky Brooklyn before adopting New England, a refresher may be useful. Dour old Yankees will know the story from earliest childhood, but since we rely for early weather history on the Pilgrims' accounts, we should try to visualize the New World as they did.

You can admire someone without liking him, and that's the way I feel when I read about the Pilgrims or read their journals. H. L. Mencken defined Puritanism as "the haunting fear that someone, somewhere, may be happy." O.K., he may have overstated it, but it's pretty certain that good times were not high on the list of Puritan priorities. Their idea of a peak experience seemed to be going to church to have their toes curled by a sermon on how a wrathful God found sinners more disgusting than horseflies with running sores and was going to pull out their arms and legs one by one before tossing them into eternal fire. I'm not a theologian, but as verbal entertainment I'd have to rate that even lower than Howard Cosell.

There are historical figures that you can imagine talking with enjoyably: a day with Thomas Jefferson, a night with Catherine the Great—there must have been some reason why she got the name. But can you imagine spending a day in Boston with Cotton Mather? The theatre—and by extension, the movies—would be strictly off-limits; and can you see him settling into the bleachers at Fenway to watch the Sox? To start off with, the fans behind would shout at him to take that ludicrous hat off, and I don't see the Rev. Mather tolerating much impertinence. The louts would be ordered into the stocks, and you'd have to explain that we don't have stocks or ducking chairs any more, that criminals are given two weeks paid vacation to Disneyland and issued new guns when they get out of the slammer. A visit to Harvard Square would surely lead him to cancel his membership in the alumni association. What with one thing and another, it would be a very long day. As you parted at twilight, he would probably be gracious and offer a public prayer to God to have mercy on your sniveling wormlike abscessed soul, and then you could go off to some local bar to find out what goes into a triple martini.

Now, I wouldn't go on and on about this if it weren't for the fact that the Puritans really were among the least frivolous people the world has ever seen. And there are residuals, as we say in the television business. A friend of mine who lives in a New England village enjoys his reputation as a local rake, (actually, he admits that he would enjoy the reality more than the reputation), and swears that he sees the ghost of Cotton Mather in the eyes of his neighbors when he manages to lure a sweet young thing back to his house. In our pleasure-loving modern society, we may find it hard to be sympathetic to stiff-necked Mathers and Winthrops, but after all, they didn't land in Beverly Hills, so quick repartee and a wardrobe of designer jeans weren't what was needed. But they had what it took for Plymouth.

To quote Will and Ariel Durant: "The Puritan regimen narrowed the mind but strengthened the will and the character," both of which are basic equipment if you're engaged in a struggle for survival. And, to return triumphantly to the subject of this book at a point where you were probably thinking that I had forgotten, New

England weather was waiting for them when they jumped off the Mayflower. It was something new for them, and they needed all their character and will to survive it.

The English have been complaining about their weather for centuries. One amusing recent example will show you:

A Song of the Weather, by Michael Flanders and Donald Swann

> *January brings the snow,*
> *Makes your feet and fingers glow;*
> *February's ice and sleet*
> *Freeze the toes right off your feet;*
> *Welcome March with wintry wind;*
> *Would thou wert not so unkind.*
> *April brings the sweet spring showers,*
> *On and on for hours and hours;*
> *Farmers fear unkindly May,*
> *Frost by night and hail by day;*
> *June just rains and never stops,*
> *Thirty days and spoils the crops.*
> *In July the sun is hot.*
> *Is it shining? No, it's not.*
> *August cold and dank and wet*
> *Brings more rain than any yet.*
> *Bleak September's mist and mud*
> *Is enough to chill the blood.*
> *Then October adds a gale,*
> *Wind and slush and rain and hail.*
> *Dark November brings the fog,*
> *Should not do it to a dog;*
> *Freezing wet December, then*
> *Bloody January again!*

Now, it's a very clever song (in their Angel recording "At the Drop of a Hat," Michael Flanders goes on to admit that it was "very nice yesterday, wasn't it: spring. I enjoyed that. Missed it last year; I was in the bathroom."), but as meteorology, it's a whopper, leagues beyond any weatherman's 11 P.M. fib. The English climate is notoriously changeable and definitely moist—some would call it dank—but it is extremely mild. For this, they have the Gulf Stream

17

to thank: this warmest of all ocean currents makes a convenient right turn after sweeping by our Atlantic shore and moves in close enough off the British Isles to make the weather there far warmer than you'd expect from their latitude. London, after all, is about 300 miles farther north than the very tip of Maine. In spite of location, the temperature range for Ireland and most of England is what climatologists call "oceanic," with cool summers and mild winters, and a seasonal range of about 20 degrees Fahrenheit. Strangely enough, it is a relatively uncommon climate, and if the Pilgrims had wanted to duplicate it, there are only three other places on earth where they could have gone: a small strip of the Pacific coast from northern California to Vancouver; a similar strip in Chile; or New Zealand and the southern fringe of Australia. Well, the Concorde wasn't in action then, so they settled for New England's 'continental' climate with full (not cool) summers and cold (not mild) winters, taking it on the chin at both extremes with seasonal temperature variations of 40 degrees Fahrenheit or more.

As proud as I am of the wonderful variety and perversity of weather here in the Northeast, I have to confess that climate maps will show places with even greater extremes: right here in the United States, North Dakota and northern Minnesota are capable of greater dimensions of blistering and freezing, perhaps a 70 degree seasonal range. And there are enormous tracts of Siberia where the combination of temperate summers—highs like in England—and truly arctic winters will make for seasonal differences of over 100 degrees Fahrenheit! And please remember that all of these figures refer not to the hottest versus the coldest days, but to the hottest and coldest *months* averaged over many years. All of us seasoned, hardy New Englanders have survived years which may have seen temperatures 100 degrees apart, but I don't know if even Puritan character would be much help in Siberia, where that difference might be as much as 170 degrees. I'm not a political scientist, but I'm willing to bet that the Russian way of settling Siberia would be the only way to do it.

I don't have to remind you that the Puritans didn't go about things that way. In fact, they were in the vanguard of a new way of thinking that was emerging in 16th and 17th century England. Representative government is taken for granted nowadays—whether it really occurs or not—but 300 years ago it was a radical, even subversive idea. It seems to have been a native English idea, but it didn't

have easy going even there in an age of absolute monarchs. The Puritans' concern was that the monarch's power extended to religious beliefs, and it was accepted that loyal subjects would worship in the manner their sovereign ordered them to. (It would be nice to think of our century as enlightened and superior, but the Holocaust and the Armenian Massacre are just two examples of modern man's capacity for intolerance.) Hence, the Puritans' long voyage across the Atlantic ending on Cape Cod in December.

Cape Cod in December! If a shipload of twentieth-century Puritans were to land there this year in December, they wouldn't find it greatly changed. The same raw weather, cold beyond their English experience; and they'd find the area almost as sparsely settled as did their predecessors, since nowadays most people with a few hundred dollars left on their credit lines are off in Florida or the Bahamas.

Such as it was, it was land, and after an Atlantic crossing in the fall, it looked good. William Bradford, Governor of Plymouth Plantation, tells the story of their arrival:

> "After they had injoyed faire winds and weather for a season, they were incountred many times with crosse winds, and mete with many feirce stormes, with which the shipe was shroudly shaken, and her upper works made very

19

leakie; and one of the maine beames in the midd ships was bowed and craked, which put them in some fear that the shipe could not be able to perform the vioage. . . . In sundrie of these stormes the winds were so feirce, & the seas so high, as they could not beare a knote of saile, but were forced to hull, for diverce days togither. . . . But to omite other things, (that I may be breefe) after longe beating at sea they fell with that land which is called Cape Cod; the which being made & certainly knowne to be it, they were not a little joyfull. After some deliberation had amongst them selves & with the mr. of the ship, they tacked aboute and resolved to stande for the southward (the wind & weather being faire) to finde some place about Hudsons river for their habitation. But after they had sailed that course about halfe the day, they fell amongst deangerous shoulds and roring breakers, and they were so farr intangled ther with as they conceived them selves in great danger; & the wind shrinking upon them withall, they resolved to bear up againe for the Cape, and thought them selves hapy to gett out of those dangers before night overtooke them, as by Gods providence they did. And the next day they gott into the Cape-harbor wher they ridd in saftie. . . .

Being thus arived in a good harbor and brought safe to land, they fell upon their knees and blessed the God of heaven, who had brought them over the vast & furious ocean, and delivered them from all the periles & miseries thereof, againe to set their feete on the firme and stable earth, their proper elements. . . . But hear I cannot but stay and make a pause, and stand half amased at this poore peoples presente condition; and so I thinke will the reader too, when he well considers the same. Being thus passed the vast ocean, and a sea of troubles before in their preparation (as may be remembred by that which wente before), they had now no freinds to wellcome them, nor inns to entertaine or refresh their weatherbeaten bodys, no houses or much less townes to repaire too, to seeke for succoure. It is recorded in scripture as a mercie to the apostle & his shipwraked company, that the barbarians shewed them no smale kindnes in refreshing them, but these savage barbarians, when they mette with them (as after

will appear) were readier to fill their sids full of arrows
then otherwise. And for the season it was winter, and they
that know the winters of that cuntrie know them to be
sharp & violent, & subjecte to cruell & feirce stromes,
deangerous to travill to known places, much more to serch
an unknown coast. Besids, what could they see but a
hidious & desolate wildernes, full of wild beasts and willd
men? and what multituds ther might be of them they
know not. . . . For summer being done, all things stand
upon them with a wetherbeaten face; and the whole coun-
trie, full of woods & thickets, represented a wild & savage
heiw. If they looked behind them, ther was the mighty
ocean which they had passed, and was now as a maine barr
& goulfe to seperate them from all the civill parts of the
world. . . .''

Earlier in his account, Bradford tells an anecdote that shows a
real streak of what seems like Puritan nastiness. It has nothing to do
with weather, and copying out Bradford is dangerous for my always
shaky sense of spelling, but I think it's worth a minute or two of your
time:

". . .yet according to the usual maner many were afflicted
with sea-sicknes. And I may not omite hear a spetiall
worke of Gods providence. Ther was a proud & very pro-
fane yonge man, one of the sea-men, of a lustie, able
body, which made him the more hauty; he would allway
be contemning the poore people in their sicknes, & cursing
them dayly with greevous execrations, and did not let to
tell them, that he hoped to help to caste halfe of them over
board before they came to their jurneys end, and to make
mery with what they had; and if he were by any gently
reproved, he would curse and swear most bitterly. But it
plased God before they came halfe seas over, to smite this
yong man with a greeveous disease, of which he dyed in a
desperate maner, and so was him selfe the first that was
throwne overbord. Thus his curses light on his owne head;
and it was an astonishment to all his fellows, for they
noted it to be the just hand of God upon him.''

I don't doubt for a second that the guy was a creep, and it
couldn't have happened to a nicer person. But there's a sort of
gloating tone about the whole affair that makes me a bit uncomfort-

21

able. All the passengers did was to gently reprove him, and when God's providence takes care of matters by offing him, there isn't even any conventional piety about commending his soul to God and his body to the deep. I don't think I'd want to cross Mr. Bradford.

With that reflection on the workings of the Puritan mind, we are going to leave them for just a bit, because although we rely on them for complete early accounts of our weather, they weren't the first visitors to our shores.

Columbus Lucked Out

By common consent, the Vikings were our first visitors. Unfortunately, they left no written records. I'm not sure how interesting they would have been: these guys were *tough*, a handful of nails for breakfast, a good night's sleep lashed to the bowsprit of a boat on the high seas, that kind of thing. Although coastal Scandinavia is pretty mild—our friend the Gulf Stream at work again—by the time they had spent several generations on the North Atlantic around Greenland, they would probably not have been too impressed by any weather Newfoundland could throw at them. It would probably take a hurricane just to get their attention.

So our records have to start with Christopher Columbus. He never did come far north, but he spent a lot of time around the Bahamas, where some very interesting northeastern weather is spawned.

As it happens, on his first voyage he didn't see any of it. Which was certainly lucky for him. He was cruising in the West Indies near the peak of the hurricane season, and he encountered no severe storms at all, let alone a hurricane. The only hint of trouble on the trip came when his little fleet was about two weeks out from the Canary Islands and "the sea made up considerably, and without wind, which astonished them." Most probably the heavy swells were due to bad weather several hundred miles distant, so his timing was excellent. The highest winds reported on the outward voyage occurred just before landfall when the northeast trades piped up in the evening to near-gale force, driving the *Nina*, the *Pinta*, and the *Santa Maria* along at a nine-knot clip toward San Salvador and destiny. Nine knots, by the way, is a terrific speed under sail, particularly at night approaching a totally unknown coast. Columbus was no faintheart.

What might have been the course of history if, in that autumn of 1492, a full-blown tropical storm had been lying in wait for Columbus's dinky little boats? They certainly would have been sent to the bottom, and the Old World would never have known what happened. Educated men then did not really believe that you were in danger of dropping off the edge of the world if you sailed too far west, but even in the great age of exploration, that sort of disappearance might have cooled enthusiasm for a while. But luck (or, as Columbus would have it, the will of God) prevailed, and in fact Columbus was able to write that "in all the Indies, I have always found weather like May." Later, he learned better.

On the trip home, early in 1493, Columbus ran into two extremely heavy storms near the Azores, and his ships were battered for days. In retrospect, the West Indies then must have seemed even more like a Paradise.

He made his second voyage in the fall of 1493, and again he lucked out by arriving in the Caribbean at the tail end of the normal hurricane season. The only important weather events on the way were a few thundersqualls that split some sails and broke a few spars. Routine business for Columbus, perhaps, but I wouldn't want to be on board.

But two years later we have a report of an interesting bit of weather in the New World, one which certainly must have caused Columbus to rethink his earlier opinion about perpetual May in the Indies. He had established a trading post, Isabela, on the north coast of Hispaniola, now the Dominican Republic. The following passage from Peter Martyr d'Anghiera's *The Decades of the New World or West India*, published in 1511, describes a day there in June 1495:

> "This same year in the month of June, they say there rose
> such a boisterous tempest of wind from the SE, as hath not
> lately been heard of. The violence hereof was such that it
> plucked up by the roots whatsoever great trees were within
> the force thereof. When this whirlwind came to the haven

of the city, it beat down to the bottom of the sea three ships which lay at anchor, and broke the cables in sunder: and that (which is the greater marvel) without any storm or roughness of the sea, only turning them three or four times about. The inhabitants also affirm that the same year the sea extended itself further into the land, and rose higher than ever it did before in the memory of man, by the space of a cubit.

"The people, therefore, muttered among themselves that our nation had troubled the elements and caused such portentous signs. These tempests of the air (which the Grecians call tiphones, that is whirl winds), they call Furacanes: which they say, do often times chance in this Island: But that neither they nor their great grandfathers ever saw such violent and furious Furacanes, that plucked up great trees by the rootes: Neither yet such surges and vehement motions of the sea, that so wasted the land, As indeed it may appear, for as much as, where soever the sea banks are near to any plain there are in manner everywhere, flourishing meadows reaching even unto the shore."

The word "furacane" is suspicious. From the account, it sounds much more like a tornado that developed in the interior of Hispaniola, and then moved in a northwesterly direction toward the shore. When it reached the harbor, the tornado would become a waterspout with great local destructiveness. The loss of the boats at this point was not critical, since Columbus had started his second voyage with 17 ships, and supply and booty fleets had started criss-crossing the Atlantic. Columbus did manage to salvage enough from the wrecked boats to build a new caravel that accompanied the *Nina* back to Spain early in 1496.

It seems clear that Columbus had learned the ways of Caribbean weather by his fourth voyage. Describing Columbus's actions on June 29, 1502, Samuel Eliot Morison writes: "Columbus had already experienced two hurricanes and recognized the portents only too well. An oily swell rolled in from the Southeast, veiled cirrus clouds tore along through the upper air, light gusty winds played over the surface of the water, low-pressure twinges were felt in his arthritic joints." Columbus headed for shelter, sending a note ashore to the governor of Santo Domingo predicting a hurricane within two days and urging him to postpone the departure of a treasure-laden fleet bound for Spain. The governor laughed at the warning, and his fleet of 29 ships set sail. Less than two days out, the fleet turned into the strait between Hispaniola and Puerto Rico; the hurricane bore down on them from the northeast, sending 25 of the ships to the bottom, 19 of them with no survivors. Only one ship was able to make the crossing to Spain: ironically, it was the one carrying gold belonging to Columbus. He himself, sheltered in the lee of the hurricane, rode it out with no serious damage. As Morison observes, "Columbus and his captains could not have done better if they had received storm warnings by radio." *(The European Discovery of America: The Southern Voyages 1492–1616.* New York: Oxford University Press, 1974)

Columbus was a marvelous sailor and navigator, and he had the instincts of a great weatherman. The fact that his fleets for the most part avoided any great calamity at the hands of the sometimes violent Caribbean weather speaks not only of his tremendous luck, but also of his ability to forecast weather. And to this day, only a fool sets sail without knowing how to read the sky.

Sad Storms and Wearisom Days — The Sixteenth Century

One hundred and fifteen years were to pass after Columbus's landfall on San Salvador until the English made a permanent settlement in the United States. The Sixteenth Century was the great age of exploration and discovery: Magellan's expedition circumnavigated the globe in 1519–22, and until the end of the century when England took a huge step toward naval supremacy with the defeat of the Spanish Armada, the major nations of Europe competed on the high seas to exploit the new lands which Columbus had found. Pope Alexander VI in 1493 decreed a Line of Demarcation 100 leagues west of the Azores, granting all lands to the west to Spain (the New World), except that Brazil slipped through on some technicality, and non-Christian lands to the east to Portugal (Africa and India). This was undoubtedly a well-meant attempt to keep peace in the Catholic family, but the Catholic church was to come upon hard times during the century, and Henry VIII, having challenged the Pope's authority on spiritual matters, was certainly not about to follow his ground rules for exploiting promising new territories. The names of the century's explorers (and sometimes brutal conquerors) make an astounding roll call: Balboa, the Cabots, Cabral, Cabrillo, Cabeze de Vaca, Champlain, Columbus, Coronado, Cortez, DeSoto, Dias, Diaz, Drake, da Gama, Hawkins, Hakluy, Hudson, Magellan, Minuit, Ponce de Leon, Pizarro, Raleigh, Vespucci.

In keeping with the papal bull establishing the Line of Demarcation, the Spaniards provided most of the traffic towards America. Their luck wasn't up to Columbus's old level, since there are reports of Spanish fleets being lost in 1545, 1551, 1553, 1554, and 1559. Since these dates are well before the English discovered how profitable piracy could be, we must suspect that weather was the culprit in these disappearances.

And it's interesting to note that during this century the weather had a great deal to do with the establishment of settlements and the success or failure of national ambitions. For example: the founding of

St. Augustine as a Spanish settlement owes something to a hurricane. In 1565, the French and Spanish were squaring off near St. Augustine to see who would get to massacre the other. The French, led by Jean Ribant, sailed to attack the Spanish fortifications, but a storm caught the fleet and sent the ships to the bottom along with most of the attackers. The Spanish immediately retaliated by attacking and massacring the weakened French garrison, and so a tropical storm, possibly a hurricane, determined the political fate of Florida's east coast.

And the ill-fated English attempts to found a colony farther north were discouraged by storms and the lack of sheltered harbors. Sir Humphrey Gilbert's 1583 expeditions ended in failure—and his death in a storm off the Azores. His half-brother, Sir Walter Raleigh, had accompanied Gilbert on an earlier expedition, and was to be the driving force in subsequent colonizing efforts around North Carolina. In 1584, his navigators brought back rave reviews about Roanoke Island in the intracoastal sound not far from a later historic site, Kitty Hawk. Raleigh immediately dispatched a colonizing expedition which landed there in August, 1585. The next June, Sir Francis Drake arrived offshore, but "there arose a great storm (which they said was extraordinary and very strange) and lasted three days together, and put our fleet in great danger." Sir Ralph Lane, the leader of the colony, related in his history of the expedition that "our ships were forced to put to sea. The weather was so sore and the storme so great that our anchors would not hold, and no ship of them all but either broke or lost their anchors. And our ship the *Primrose* broke an anchor of 250 lbs. weight. All the time we were in this country, we had thunder and rain with hailstones as big as hen's eggs. There were great spouts at the seas as though heaven and earth would have met." The combination of the storm and Indian hostility caused Drake to evacuate the settlers and take them back to England.

In 1587, however, Raleigh sent another colonizing expedition, and again they met with a great storm. "There arose such a tempest at northeast, that our admiral (Drake), then riding out of the harbor, was forced to cut his cables, and put to sea, where he lay beating off and on six days before he could come to us again. . . ." John White, the expedition leader, left a small group of colonists to winter over on Roanoke Island and returned to England, intending to return with supplies and more settlers.

However, other matters were more pressing. 1588 saw the battle of the Spanish Armada, and it was not until 1591 that White was able to return to Roanoke Island. As usual, "we had very foul weather, with much rain, thundering, and great spouts, which fell around us, high unto our ships." The colonists had disappeared, and further bad weather prevented a thorough search. Their fate has remained one of the great mysteries in colonial history.

The season of 1591 demonstrates that whatever else may have changed in the last 400 years, it hasn't been the weather: hurricanes were as frequent then as they are now. An expedition visited the Carolina shore in August 1591 and once again had to contend with a strong northeast gale: "For at this time the wind at Northeast and direct unto the harbor so great a gale, that the sea broke extremely on the bar, and the tide went very forcibly at the entrance." Out on the Atlantic no fewer than four major storms occured in four weeks during August and September, with the destruction of at least 27 ships reported. The Grand Fleet making its annual treasure run from Havana to Spain was caught in one of these storms and over 500 sailors went to the bottom with most of their loot.

These few examples of sixteenth-century storms show that the hurricane posed a major problem to those bent on exploration, treasure seeking, and settlement. No doubt a thorough search of Spanish archives and British Admiralty records would reveal many more hurricanes playing havoc with men and ships on the sea. But in the absence of any permanent English settlement in America during this century, meteorological data for the shoreline will always remain sketchy.

From 1620 on, records become progressively more detailed—although the earliest ones, as you will see, more than make up for the lack of precise millibar readings by their apocalyptic tone. So we're going to catalogue the outstanding weather events that have occurred in the northeast since the Puritan settlement. Almost all of these events caused a great deal of destruction and misery, because when the weather gets ornery, big things happen. However, I think you'll find some humor here too, especially in some of the early writings.

Wound Like a Withe —
The Seventeenth Century

Having established that there was indeed a great deal of weather activity even before the advent of English settlement, let's skip ahead to the early Colonial periods where the records become more complete and the descriptions more wonderful. But just imagine how terrible these mighty weather events must have been for the colonists who, by today's standards, had the most primitive of shelters and whose entire belongings and means of livelihood could easily be totally wiped out by severe weather. And these early settlers had to contend with some pretty violent stuff, one the worst of which was. . .

The Great Colonial Hurricane (1635)—Rev. Increase Mather in his *Remarkable Providences,* a review of early natural and supernatural events in New England, thought he had heard ''of no storm more dismal than the great hurricane which was in August 1635.''

This was apparently the greatest meteorological event of the colonial period in New England, coming only 15 years after the settlement of Plymouth Plantation and in the fifth year of the Massachusetts Bay Colony. It would be 180 years before another great hurricane of similar importance would strike the area with equal force — The Great September Gale of 1815.

Perhaps the historical stature of the 1635 event owes its prominence to the unusual severity of the storm itself, since the accounts of whole forests being leveled would indicate that it was a hurricane of exceedingly great force. The Great Colonial Hurricane had two able eyewitnesses whose contemporary writings form the solid foundation upon which most of the history of early New England has been based: John Winthrop of Massachusetts Bay Colony and William Bradford of Plymouth Plantation.

John Winthrop kept a running journal of the prinicpal events in the Boston area. Although his manuscript was available to colonial writers, it was not published in full until the early Nineteenth Century as *The History of New England from 1630 to 1649.*

Winthrop's account of the Great Colonial Hurricane remains the best source and reveals some essential details as to the meteorological character of this celebrated storm:

> Aug. 16. The wind having blown hard at S. and S.W. a week before, about midnight it came up at N.E. and blew with such violence, with abundance of rain, that it blew down many hundreds of trees, near the towns, overthrew some houses, and drove the ships from their anchors. The Great Hope, of Ipswitch, being about four hundred tons, was driven aground at Mr. Hoffe's Point, and brought back again presently by N.W. wind, and ran on shore at Charlestown. About eight of the clock the wind came about to N.W. very strong, and, it being then about high water, by nine the tide had fallen three feet. Then it began to flow again about one hour, and rose about two or three feet, which was conceived to be, that the sea was grown so high abroad with a N.E. wind, that, meeting with the ebb, it forced it back again. This tempest was so far at Cape Sable, but to the south more violent, and made a double tide on all that coast . . . The tide rose at Naragansett fourteen feet higher than ordinary, and drowned eight Indians flying from their wigwams.

William Bradford's *Of Plymouth Plantation* contributes some more interesting notes on this famous storm:

> This year, the 14th or 15th of August (being Saturday) was such a mighty storm of wind and rain as none living in these parts, either English or Indians, ever saw. Being like, for the time it continued, to those hurricanes and typhoons that writers make mention of in the Indies. It began in the morning a little before day, and grew not by degrees but came with violence in the beginning, to the great amazement of many. It blew down sundry houses and uncovered others. Divers vessels were lost at sea and many more in extreme danger. It caused the sea to swell to the south wind of this place about 20 foot right up and down, and made many of the Indians to climb into trees for their safety. It took off the boarded roof of a house which belonged to this plantation at Manomet and floated it to another place, the posts still standing in the ground. And if it had continued long without the shifting of the

wind, it is like it would have drowned some part of the country. It blew down many hundred thousands of trees, turning up the stronger by roots and breaking the higher pine trees off in the middle. And the tall young oaks and walnut trees of good bigness were wound like a withe, very strange and fearful to behold. It began in the southeast a parted toward the south and east, and veered sundry ways, but the greatest force of it here was from the former quarters. It continued not (in the extremity) above five or six hours but the violence began to abate. The signs and marks of it will remain this hundred years in these parts where it was sorest. The moon suffered a great eclipse the second night after it.

From these two accounts, we can roughly guess that the center of this hurricane tracked across upper Narragansett Bay closer to Providence, through the Massachusetts counties of Bristol and Plymouth, and entered Massachusetts Bay some 20 miles south of Boston. Interestingly, this was the same approximate track as that taken by two other "killer" hurricanes: the Great Atlantic Hurricane in 1944 and Edna in 1955.

The onslaught of this hurricane came at a season when a number of ships were enroute to Massachusetts Bay carrying new settlers and much-needed goods to the infant communities. The Great Hurricane caused many shipwrecks and several near-disasters.

The Triple Storms (1638)—Winthrop described two noteworthy eastern New England storms in the year 1638. On August 13, "in the night was a very great tempest, or hiracano at S.W. which drove a ship on the ground at Charlestown, and broke down the windmill there, and did much other harm."

Eight weeks later another storm of probable tropical origin brushed the New England coast, to be followed by still a third much farther offshore. Winthrop relates: "Oct 5—Being the third day of the week and two days before the change, the wind having blown at N.E. all day, and rainy in the night, was a mighty tempest, and withal the highest tide, which has been since coming into this country; but through the good providence of God, it did little harm. About fourteen days after (Oct. 19) the wind having been at N.W. and then calm here, came in the greatest eastern sea, which had been in our time. Mr. Peirce (who came in a week after) had at that time a very great tempest three days at N.E.''

Confirmation of the first of these late season hurricanes will be found in the writings of John Jocelyn. In his *Two Voyages to New England* he made the following note in 1638 while at Scarborough, Maine, a coastal town just south of Portland: ''Sept 24 - Monday about 4 o'clock in the afternoon, a fearful storm of wind began to rage, called a hurricane. It is an impetuous wind that goes commonly about the compass in the space of 24 hours. It began from the N.N.W. and continued till the next morning - the greatest mischief it did us, was the wracking of our shallops, and the blowing down of many trees, in some places a mile together.''

It is evident that the season of 1638 was prolific in the production of hurricanes.

John Winthrop's Sudden Gust (1643)—This intriguing storm occurred in present Essex County in northeastern Massachusetts and in coastal New Hampshire. The date was July 15. The complete Winthrop Journal entry follows:

> July 15. There arose a sudden gust at N.W. so violent for half an hour, as it blew down multitudes of trees. It lifted up their meeting house at Newbury, the people being in it. It darkened the air with dust, yet through God's great mercy it did no hurt, but only killed one Indian with the fall of a tree. It was straight between Linne and Hampton.

The places mentioned are separated by about 35 miles and lie almost on a due north-south line.

Whether this was a true tornado with a northerly path requiring a half hour to run its course, or whether it was a line squall striking all places at about the same time and blowing strong for half an hour, must be the reader's own decision after reading the scanty descriptive material above. There remains the possibility that a severe line squall struck the places, and a small whirlwind developed in the vicinity of Newbury at the time that the squall line passed.

Strange News from Virginia: The Dreadful Hurry Cane (1667)—A tremendous hurricane in the summer of 1667 was a major event in Virginia's early history. The main source of information comes from a contemporary pamphlet, *Strange News from Virginia, being a true relation of the great tempest in Virginia,* which was published in London sometime before the end of the year 1667. The Virginia account follows:

> The Copy of a Letter from Virginia, Containing the Relation of a Violent Hurricane, which happened the 27th of August and continued (without intermission) twelve days together.
>
> Sir,
> Having this opportunity, I cannot but acquaint you with the Relation of a very strange Tempest which hath been in these parts (with us called a Hurricane) which began Aug. 27 and continued with such Violence, that it overturned many Houses, burying in the Ruins much Goods and many people, beating to the ground such as were any wayes employed in the Fields, blowing many Cattle that were near the Sea or Rivers, into them, whereby unknown numbers have perished, to the great affliction of all people, few having escaped who have not suffered in their persons or Estates, much Corn was blown away, and great quantities of Tobacco have been lost, to the great damage of many, and utter undoing of others. Neither did it end here, but the Trees were torn up by the roots, and in many places whole Woods blown down, so that they cannot go from Plantation to Plantation.

Another account of the storm is given in a letter from Secretary Thomas Ludwell to Lord Berkeley.

> This poore Country . . . is now reduced to a very miserable condition by a continual course of misfortune. In April . . . we had a most prodigious storm of hail, many of them as big as turkey eggs, which destroyed most of our young mast and cattle. On the fifth of June following came the Dutch upon us, and did so much mischief that we shall never recover our reputations . . . There was not gone till it fell to raining and continued for 40 days together, which spoiled much of what the hail had left of our English grain. But on the 27th of August followed the most dreadful Hurry Cane that ever the colony groaned under . . . . It was accompanied with a most violent raine, but no thunder. The night of it was the most dismal time I ever knew or heard of, for the wind and rain raised so confused a noise, mixed with the continual cracks of falling houses . . . . Had the lightning accompanied it we could have believed nothing else from such a confusion but that all the elements were at strife, which of them should do most towards the reduction of the creation into a Second Chaos. . . . But then morning came and the sun risen it would have comforted us after such a night, had it not lighted to us the ruins of our plantation, of which I think not one escaped. The nearest computation is at least 10,000 houses blown down, all the Indian grain laid flat on the ground, all the Tobacco in the fields torn to pieces and most of that which was in the houses perished with them. The fences about the corn fields were either blown down or beaten to the ground by trees which fell upon them and before the owners could repair them the hogs & cattle got in and in most places devoured much of what the storm had left.

By any standards, this must have been one hell of a storm, and it probably took the Virginia settlers years to recover from it. Imagine coming all the way from Western Europe to build a new society (mostly based on trade in tobacco) and getting smacked almost back into a "Second Chaos." To us modern and enlightened folk the descriptions are almost amusing, but still we have to feel desperately sorry for the people who suffered from these storms.

Violent Hurricane (1671)—This "violent hurricane" was almost certainly a tornado, and was reported by one Rev. William Adams. Following his graduation from Harvard College in the Class of 1671, the travels of Rev. Adams apparently took him to the vicinity of Rehoboth, a settlement on the border of Massachusetts and Rhode Island about seven miles east of Providence. (This is the same area where a sizable tornado with a track of 25 miles would pass on August 30, 1838.) A diary entry under the date of October 26, 1671 reports:

> I rid out with some others to see the strange effects of a violent hurricane that had been on the - of Aug. about a mile and a half from Rehoboth, carrying about 20 rods in breadth, tearing up by the roots, or breaking the bodies of almost all trees within its compass saving only some small and low ones, and it is thought in all probability to have gone 15 miles in length.

The New England Hurricane (1675)—Just forty years after the Great Hurricane of 1635, a storm with many similar characteristics swept the New England coastal regions, including Connecticut, Rhode Island, and Massachusetts.

At New London a "dreadful storm of wind and rain at East" occurred in August according to the journal of Simon Bradstreet which chronicled the outstanding events in Connecticut and New England. At nearby Stonington many ships were wrecked and "much loss of hay and corn. Multitudes of trees blown down." Peter Easton in Rhode Island, after recalling the hurricane of 1635, related that "much the like storm blew down our windmill and did much harm."

The occurrence of the 1675 storm was noted by John Hull of Boston who wrote in his diary under August 29: "a very violent storm, that exceedingly blew down the Indian corn and the fruit of trees; did much spoil on the warves, and among the ships and vessels in Boston, to value supposed a thousand pounds."

The evidence of trees blown down along the Connecticut shore and Hull's description of damage at Boston would place the 1675 storm high on the list of New England's most destructive hurricanes, just a notch below the great storms of 1635, 1815, 1938, and 1944.

A Whirl-wind at Cambridge (1680)—Eyewitness accounts helped Rev. Increase Mather describe (in his *Remarkable Providences)* a whirlwind or small tornado which passed through Cambridge on July 18, 1680. Its track was rather close to that of a much larger storm which was to move through West Cambridge on August 22, 1851. The earlier disturbance seemed to have all the characteristics of a true tornado:

> Samual Stone of Cambridge in New England does declare and testifie, that July 8, 1680, about two of clock in the afternoon, he being with his young son in the field, the wind then southerly, he observed a cloud in the north-west in opposition to the wind, which caused a singing noise in the air; and the wind increased till the whirl-wind came, which began in the meadow near where he was, though then it was not so violent as it proved afterwards. As it passed by him it sucked up and whirled about the hay that was within the compass of it; it passed from him towards his house over a hill, tearing down several trees as it went along; and, coming to his barn, carried off a considerable part of the roof (about twenty-four foot one way, and thirty the other), which fell near the dwelling-house where people were, yet could not its fall be heard by them (yet it was so great that it was heard by some a mile off) by reason of the great rushing noise of the wind. Matthew Bridge, who was [also] an eye-witness of what happened, declares that he observed a thick cloud coming along his father's field before his house, as to appearance very black; in the inside of the cloud as it passed over him, there seemed to be a light pillar, as he judged about eight or ten foot diameter, which seemed to him like a screw or solid body. Its motion was continually circular, which turned about the rest of the cloud. It passed along upon the ground, tearing all before it, bushes by the roots, yea the earth itself, removing old trees as they lay along on the earth, and stones of a great magnitude, some of which could not be found again. . . . The cloud itself was filled with stones, bushes, boughs, and other things that it had taken up from the earth, so that the top and sides of the cloud seemed like a green wood. . . . The above-said Matth. Bridge, and a boy with him, endeavoured to run to the

house, but were prevented by the storm, so that they were necessitated to ly flat upon the ground behind some bushes, and this thick cloud and pillar passed so near them as almost to touch their feet, and with its force bent the bushes down over them, and yet their lives were preserved. John Robbins, a servant man, was suddenly slain by this storm, his body being much bruised, and many bones broken by the violence thereof.

Dreadful Havock (1682)—Rev. Mather received two letters from fellow clergymen reporting what was obviously a tornado. The date was June 18, 1682, and the funnel apparently originated west of the Housatonic River and north of Fairfield in southern Connecticut. It then passed in an easterly direction over the northern part of Stratford, across Milford, and through New Haven where it moved into Long Island Sound. The first letter from Isreal Chauncey said, in part:

> As to that great storm of thunder, lightning & raine, my wife and I were on our journey that day from Norwalk to Stamford to give a visit to our good friend Mrs. Bishop. By that time we were com to a little house in the mid way, set up about a month before, the storme began: & before we could well get in the furniture of our horses; other company with us; the storme grew to that violence that had we been but a quarter of a mile from the house we could not have reached it without great hazard of life. But God brought us to that shelter just in the nick of tyme, where we stayed some houres till the storme was over, hoping it would hold up: but a little raine we had in the rest of our journey to Stamford; & did observe many vast & green Oakes blowne downe & torne up by the roots; som in the road, that stopt up the way. But some dayes after, on our returne we found a dredfull destruccon of trees, all the way from Stamford, from towne to towne, & especially in Milford in the rode & neere it, heapes of mighty Oakes turned up by the roots; but not many afterwards in the rest of the way to N.H. [New Haven].

The second letter, from one William Jones, reported:

> The storme reached Stratford, Milford, Fairfield, N. Haven; and it was very violent in every one of these places,

but especially in Milford, where three barnes were blown down by it, and one house new-built, that was fourty foot in length, well enclosed, was moved from the foundation at one corner, near two foot and a halfe: but the greatest strength of the Storme was about six miles above Stratford, as is evident by the dreadful havock that it there made, for the compasse of halfe a mile in bredth scarce a tree left standing, which is not greatly shaken by the storme. . . . The very noise of the wind in the woodes was such that those that were in it could not heare the fall of a tree a few rods from them. Great limbs of trees were carried like feathers in the air: Many that were at worke in the woodes were in great danger, [and] had no way to preserve themselves but by running into open planes where there were no trees.

Great Flood (1683)—Increase Mather in his *Remarkable Providences* stated that a hurricane took place in Virginia at the same time that a vast flood inundated the Connecticut Valley. Another report on about the same day related that at Stonington on the Connecticut shore of Long Island Sound there was a "great storme that blasted all the trees." From New Hampshire we hear "exceeding high tide and stormy weather." Undoubtedly, Mather's Virginia hurricane moved into New England and released a tremendous amount of rain, resulting in heavy flooding in the river valleys, most noteably the Connecticut. About that storm, and the floods that year, he says:

Some remarkable land floods have likewise happened in New England. Nor is that which came to pass this present year to be here wholy passed over in silence. In the spring time, the great river Connecticut used to overflow, but this year it did so after midsummer, and that twice; for, July 30, 1683, a considerable flood unexpectedly arose, which proved detrimental to many in that colony. But on August 13 a second and more dreadful flood came: the water were then observed to rise twenty-six foot above the usual boundaries: the grass in the meadows, also the English grain, was carried away before it; the Indian corn, by the long continuance of the waters, is spoiled, so that the four river towns viz. Windsor, Hartford, Weathersfield, Middle-Town are extreme sufferers. They write from thence, that some who had hundreds of bushels of corn in the morning, at night had not one peck left for their families to live on.

He goes on to say "there are those think that the last comet, and those more rare conjunctions of the superior planets happening this year, have had a natural influence into the mentioned inundations."

Wow! What a thing for weathermen to fall back on. When their prediction of "hot and sunny" turns out to be cold and drab, it's Jupiter aligning with Mars. Or hot damn - blame that unpredicted snowstorm on Khoutek. Everyone used to claim that unusual weather was caused by atomic bomb testing and Communist conspiracy; but Mather, writing 300 years ago, has finally given us an answer to those unpredicted weather happenings.

The Great Storm (1693)—Terrible storms do not always have to leave disastrous results. For example, what was possibly a hurricane occurred on October 29, 1693 at the Kingdom of Acomack (now known as the Delmarva peninsula between Chesapeake Bay and the Atlantic Ocean). A Mr. Scarburgh submitted a letter to the Royal Society in London describing the storm: "There happened a most violent storme in Virginia, which stopped the Course of the ancient Chanels, and made some where there never were any: So that betwixt the Bounds of Virginia and Newcastle in Pennsylvania, on the Seaboard side, are many navigable Rivers for Sloops and small Vessels." It is also thought that this same storm opened the Fire Island Cut, east of New York City, thereby giving Great South Bay access to the sea.

The Hard Winter (1697-98)—Many New Englanders cringe at thoughts of harsh winters over the past fifteen or twenty years, and recall with awe the fact that roads were closed for a few days, heating bills skyrocketed, and snow removal was erratic and inefficient. But the Hard Winter (as it came to be known) was legendary and its reputation for severity survived for many years. "The terriblest winter for continuance of frost and snow, and extremity of cold, that was ever known." Between November 20 and April 9, thirty-one snowstorms were reported. The Charlestown, Massachusetts, ferry was frozen in for six weeks, and a 42-inch snow depth was reported at Cambridge. And they didn't even have snowplows!

The Stormy Autumn (1698)—This was a stormy autumn along the New England shore. We are indebted to John Pike of Dover, New Hampshire, who maintained a diary of events from 1678 to 1709; for many of these years he had an addenda called "Observable Seasons" which gave a brief summary of the outstanding weather happenings. The successive storms chronicled for 1698 came within the normal hurricane season and might have been of tropical origin:

> October 10—Was a violent south-east storm that blew down many fences & Shattered tops of some houses and barns.
> October 23—A violent north-east storm produced ye like effects, nearer ye sea it fell rain, higher up in the country snow.
> October 29—A violent north-east storm – melted snow – caused freshets higher than ever known.

The same sequence of events would occur again in October, 1783. Obviously, the eleven months from November, 1697 to October, 1698 were pretty hairy from a weather standpoint. Today, most of the population would probably move to Florida or Arizona after such a siege, but these hardy colonists had no such choice. They must have been pretty tough.

Prodigious Gusts and Deep Snows — The Eighteenth Century

At the end of every century, most people expect dramatic changes to take place, and their lives to be changed in one way or another. The weather, however, does not pay much attention to the silly numbers that man puts on the seasonal patterns, and you can be sure that the eighteenth century had its share of heavy stuff, beginning with. . . .

The Year of the Big Winds (1703)—The early years of the Eighteenth Century brought memorable storms to both sides of the Atlantic Ocean. It was on December 7–8, 1703 that the *Great Storm* raged across the British Isles creating what was probably the most powerful wind force ever experienced in the modern annals of southern England. The storm's frame has been recorded and immortalized by its historian, Daniel Defoe, whose *The Storm: or A Collection of the most remarkable Casualties under Disasters which happened in the late Dreadful Tempest, both by Sea and Land,* published in 1704, is a meteorological classic.

A month and a week earlier another severe storm had struck the Middle Atlantic coast of America; some writers have associated these two as parts of the same storm system, but the time interval separating them is much too long, from a meteorological point of view, to associate them together as emanations of the same disturbance.

The main account of the American hurricane of October 18, 1703 is taken from printed excerpts of the manuscript diary of Rev. Sandel, a Swedish clergyman then living along the shores of the lower Delaware River: "On the 18th of the same in the evening, a hurricane arose which caused great damage. In Maryland and Virginia, many vessels were cast away, several driven to sea, and no more heard of. Ten tobacco houses belonging to one man were overturned. In Philadelphia, the roof of a house was torn off. A great number of large trees blown down." Rev. Sandel also mentioned that an unusual early season snowstorm had taken place just eight days before the hurricane. The *Journal of Rev. John Pike* of Dover, New Hampshire, also mentioned the early snow of 1703 and further remarked:

"Oct. 17, 18 and 19 very cold storm of rain." Though there is no mention of wind damage in New England, the track of the storm probably moved close to the shore and induced a cold northeasterly air flow over New England.

The Stormy Season (1706)—The Boston *News Letter* carried several accounts of storms in the late season of 1706. Meager information on a mid-October storm hints that it might have been similar to the 1938 hurricane in respect to causing floods in eastern New York and western New England.

> New York, Oct. 14—We have great rains here and mighty Floods; They write from Albany, that the late great Rains has caused the greatest Flood there that ever was known; they say that Rensleers Island was 6-foot under water and that it drowned their low lands.
>
> New Haven, Oct. 16—On the 14, 15, and 16th days of this instant, there fell an excessive rain, which caused an unusual flood in the Connecticut River, which was accompanied by a very hard Gale of Wind between the East and South, to the great damage of the people on that river, it covered all the meadows, and carried away near 1000 loads of hay, besides the loss of the second crop of grass, and other losses."

Another blow two weeks later would appear to have been well offshore. The Boston *News Letter* later carried an account of a severe storm which had raged offshore from Virginia to New England on or about November 6, 1706. An England-bound fleet sailing from New England was scattered by a great wind when two days at sea. A Virginia fleet, also sailing about the same time, met a storm soon after its departure. Fourteen of the ships were known to have foundered, and others were given up for lost. The first news of these twin disasters was apparently carried back from England by a ship arriving at Boston in March 1707.

New London Hurricane (1713)—On August 30, 1713, a violent storm of rain and wind was followed by a "Hurricane which blew down several buildings and fruit trees such as hath not been known. It blasted or withered ye leaves like frost, though warm weather."

The 1716 Hurricane—A violent wind and rain storm visited eastern Massachusetts on October 24–25, 1716, apparently the western part of a severe gale which swept the shipping channels offshore with devastating effect. Samuel Sewall, the eminent Boston diarist, noted "many trees, fences, etc. blown down." Out at Truro on Cape Cod, Moses Pain, witnessing the storm, marked in his diary: "Oct. 14, 1716—being Lords Day, and an excessive wind so great that there was no meeting in Eastham." The hurricane was also noted on Martha's Vineyard where Rev. William Homes called it a "violent storm of wind and rain." From the New Hampshire post of Piscataqua came the report: "Since the last great storm we have 6 or 7 vessels come in here, and every one has lost their masts."

The Great Snow (1717)—This was probably New England's most legendary snowstorm. Actually, it consisted of four separate storms, two major and two minor, lasting from February 27 to March 7. Reported snow depths ranged from three feet in the Boston area to five feet and more in Maine and New Hampshire. Houses collapsed and animals perished, but Cotton Mather, in his report to the Royal Society of London told about sheep buried under drifts for 28 days being dug out alive. I think we can assume that transportation and travel in New England came to a complete halt for quite awhile.

The Great Tide (1723)—On March 7, Mather described a "tide and storm of uncommon circumstances." Apparently a strong nor'easter arrived at the time of spring tide, driving water 20 feet higher than known before. In Boston, wharves were swept away and streets were flooded for a brief period.

The Great Gust (1724)—Though the severe storm which struck the Chesapeake Bay area of Virginia and Maryland in August 1724 produced a long-lasting impression, very few meteorological details have been preserved. The *Virginia Gazette* twenty years later in describing a storm remarked: "The like has not been known in the Memory of Man, not even in the great Gust in the year 1724."

The occurrence of the Great Gust in Virginia has been definitely dated through a letter of Lt. Governor Drysdale to the Council of Trade and Plantations in London. Drysdale comments: ". . . had it not that violent storm which happened the 23rd of August almost wholly destroyed all of the tobacco on the ground . . . nor has the storm affected only one crop of tobacco, but the country suffers very much for want of corn. . . .''

A contemporary witness, John Custis, who lived on the James River, wrote with a date line August 23: ''We have had such a violent flood of rain and prodigious gust of wind that the like I do not believe never happened since the universal deluge.'' He added that most of the tobacco in the region had been destroyed, some homes wrecked, and several vessels driven ashore.

If the dating of the Virginia hurricane is correct, there must have been a second one which followed closely on the heels of the Great Gust. There are two bits of contemporary evidence for this. First, Governor Nicholson of South Carolina wrote to the Duke of Newcastle on Sept. 5, 1724: ''We had on ye 17th instant a sort of hurricane which I thank God did no damage to the shipping here, but ye violence of the rain and wind I hear hath damnified some of the Indian corn and rice and ye flood hath ruined some of the bridges.'' Secondly, a dispatch in the Boston press from Rhode Island described the arrival of a ship which had lost both masts in a great storm offshore on the 30th. The continued rains in Virginia would give credence to the belief that at least two tropical storms were involved in the floods of 1724.

A Great Rain and a Horrible Wind (1727)—The hurricane of 1727 lived long in the memory of residents of eastern Massachusetts. The Rev. Samuel Phillips preached a sermon in December, 1727 about the calamities which beset New England that year: ''Then the Lord sent a great rain and horrible wind; whereby much hurt was done, both on the water and on the land.''

The *Weekly News Letter* of Boston in September carried the following account:

> On Saturday last the 16th Instant, we had here a violent storm of wind and rain, which lasted till about midnight, whereby great damage was done to the wharfs and shipping in the harbor, as also to the fruits of the earth, and to many buildings: Many trees blown up by the roots, and chimnies blown down: a kitchen chimney of Mr. Jacob Sheaf's at the bottom of the Common, blew down and

beat on the roof, which killed a child of about 7 years of age, wounded two others, and broke the bone of Mrs. Sheaf's leg. But it is pleasant to behold very early in the next morning, which lasted a considerable length of time, a very fair rain-bow, a token of the covenant between God and the earth that the waters shall no more become a flood to destroy all flesh."

From Marblehead came a more enlightening meteorological report: "The last Saturday we had a most terrible storm of wind and rain, such as has not been known among us, which began about noon and continued to about twelve at night. The wind was at N.E. and N.E. by N. which brought in a very high tide. . . . It blew up many trees by the roots. Great damage occurred among the ships and vessels."

The hurricane also struck coastal Connecticut and Rhode Island a severe blow. At New London, according to the farmer-diarist Joshua Hempstead, the northeast wind was accompanied by rain, and many trees were uprooted. At Swanzey on Narragansett Bay, perhaps closer to the center, "it blew up trees by the roots in abundance; blew down several chimneys, and blew off the roof of a house, and blew sundry vessels on shore."

The center of the storm must have passed over some land area of southeastern Massachusetts. The east-northeast wind at Boston would indicate a close proximity as would the severe destruction in Essex County. The evidence of trees torn up by the roots from Connecticut to Cape Ann, northeast of Boston, would indicate that the storm packed a full hurricane punch even on its western side.

Hard Winter (1740-41)—This second so-called Hard Winter was considered more severe by old-timers in New England than the famous winter of 1697–98, with more snow and a longer freeze-up. There were three bad winter periods: in November, in early January, and from mid-February to mid-March. In Boston, the harbor was frozen solid for 30 straight days and the Charlestown ferry was out of operation for 10 weeks. In central Connecticut, the snow was three feet deep for most of the winter. At Ashburnham, Mass., there was still 30 inches of snow on the ground on April 10.

Benjamin Franklin's Eclipse Hurricane (1743)—This storm, which raced northward along the Atlantic Coast on November 2, deserves a unique place in the annals of American meteorology. Not only was this the first tropical storm in America to be measured accurately by scientific instruments, but it also provided Benjamin Franklin with a key to unlock for the first time the secret of a storm's forward movement.

John Winthrop, professor of Natural Philosophy at Harvard College, had commenced a meteorological register at Cambridge in 1742. His notation for November 2, 1743 follows: "N.E. by N. worst in years – great damage on land as well as sea. Barometer 29.35". Tide within 4" of 20 years ago. Storm abated about 7 P.M. Barometer lowest at 2 P.M."

The following informative account appeared in the *Boston Evening Post:*

> Last Friday night, soon after a total and visible eclipse of the Moon (which began about nine and ended past one o'clock) came on a storm of wind and rain, which continued all the following day with great violence, and the wind being at N.E., the tide was raised as high within a few inches, as that remarkable one about 20 years ago: And as Dr. Ames had given no hint in his almanack of these events, (For which Omissions let him answer) which might have put the people on guard, the greatest damage by far has been done here, that was ever known to be done by a storm in the memory of man.

The Boston *Post Boy* describes the damage about the harbor:

> The wind being excessive high vast damage was done to the wharves and shipping, some vessels that got loose were drove ashore higher up than was ever known before, and several small vessels were cast upon the wharves and boats floated into the streets. . . . Tis impossible to enumerate all the particulars of the terrible effects of this storm or estimate the damage sustained by it.

The editor of the Boston *News Letter* added:

> At noon the wind seemed to blow in prodigous gusts, and with the greatest fierceness and brought in an exceeding high tide, which overflowed most of our wharves, and

came up into several streets higher than has been known
for these twenty years past.

The storm also was violent in New Hampshire. The tide rose very
high and overflowed the wharves. At Newbury much damage was
done, as usual, to the fields and salt marshes.

Southward along the coast the disturbance appeared earlier. This
stormy weather greatly dismayed Benjamin Franklin in Philadelphia
since he had planned to observe the scheduled eclipse of the moon
that evening, but was prevented from doing so by the cloud cover.
Later he wrote his brother at Boston about his disappointment,
assuming that he, too, had been prevented from seeing the spectacle
since the cloud-bearing wind current seemed to be moving from the
northeast. Much to his surprise, Franklin later learned that the eclipse
had been seen at Boston, but that clouds arrived and a northeast wind
set in soon afterwards, to be followed by a violent storm. Franklin

noted the difference in time between the onset of the storm at
Philadelphia and Boston and reasoned that it must have been the
same disturbance, traveling from southwest to northeast against the
current of the surface wind. He embodied this thought later in a letter to Jared Eliot in 1750, and this is generally regarded as the first
tangible progress in trying to understand what the next century
would refer to as the "law of storms."

In later years there was much speculation as to just what day and
to what storm Franklin had made reference since his letter was in-
definite on this point. In 1833 his great-grandson Alexander Bache
traced by astronomical calculations the occurrence of the eclipse and
correctly dated the storm. And as late as 1906 some comments on the
same subject appeared in the publications of the American
Philosophical Society to establish definitely that Franklin was the
originator of this basic principle of storm movement.

Winter of the Deep Snows (1747-48)—Wouldn't the ski area operators of today go wild over a winter like this. But then again, probably nobody could get to the mountains to enjoy it. Between Christmas Day, 1747 and the beginning of April, 1748, New England was hit with a total of 30 snowstorms, giving an uprecedented snow cover of five to six feet in Portland, Maine and four to five feet in Boston. There is no report from the inland mountains, but one could estimate the snowfall to be above 15 to 20 feet. Thankfully, the spring of 1748 began slowly and carefully, and the region was spared excessive flooding from a rapid thaw.

The Pepperell Tornado (1748)—A powerful tornado of respectable dimensions moved over a short course through a section of Groton, Massachusetts (now known as Pepperell) in July, 1748. It continued into nearby New Hampshire, though no account of its presence in that colony has been uncovered.

An account of the Pepperell Tornado appeared in two Boston newspapers. The following letter, which appeared there, has been attributed to the Rev. Joseph Emerson, the minister of Groton West Parish.

> We had here, last Thursday, the 28th Instant, a terrible Hurricane, with shocking Thunder. The Course of the Whirlwind was from South to North, tho' often varying, sometimes bearing to the East and sometimes to the West. . . . It hath carried away a considerable part of the Roof of the Meeting-House, threw down the Fences, Stone-Walls, laid the Corn even with the Ground; the Air was fill'd with Leaves, Hay, Dust, Pieces of Timber, and Boughs of Trees of considerable bigness, for a Quarter of an Hour, which was the Time it was in passing thro' the Parish; one House which it took in its Way was garrison'd; one Side of the Garrison was thrown with great violence against the House, the other sides levell'd with the Ground, and part of the House carry'd away: There was a Woman and three small Children in the House, who were all wonderfully preserved, from receiving the least Hurt. Notwithstanding the great Desolation made among us, there was not life lost, thro' the divine Goodness, tho' many Persons were in imminent Danger. We have not yet

heard where it began; it went quite thro' the Parish; it's Impetuosity ceased near the Line between Hampshire and this Province, which is not far from us. Damage sustain'd by one man is very considerable, what in the Destruction of his Buildings, Corn, Hay, Fences, &c. he has lost above 500£.

The First Drought (1749)—The first report of a severe drought in New England occurred in the spring of 1749. Apparently there was no precipitation whatsoever from April to early July, causing crop losses and many field fires. Relief finally came on July 6, and the fall harvest was reported to be excellent.

October Hurricane (1749)—The Middle Atlantic Coast from North Carolina to New Jersey experienced a severe storm on October 18–19, 1749. The center may have moved inside Cape Hatteras, but appears to have remained a short distance offshore from Virginia northward to New Jersey and then passed close to the islands of southeastern Massachusetts and Cape Cod. At the Outer Banks of North Carolina, nine out of ten vessels who were awaiting a fair wind to put to sea were lost.

The storm struck hard at the entire lower Chesapeake Bay area "with a great gust of wind and rain" on Sunday. Near Williamsburg some houses were carried away by the flooding waters. At Hampton the water rose four feet deep in the streets; trees were torn up by the roots, other snapped off in the middle. "The like storm has not been known here in the memory of the oldest men," concluded the account.

At New York City the "violent gale" out of the east and northeast left many small craft high and dry. From Boston the *Evening Post* reported: "We had for the time it lasted as violent a gale of wind as has been known, which did considerable damage to shipping in this harbor."

It is interesting to note that Benjamin Franklin at Philadelphia had this storm under surveillance. From the fact that it was first reported in North Carolina and Virginia on the 7th and in New England on the 8th, he drew confirmation of his hypothesis that coastal storms moved from the southwest and were preceded by northeast winds.

The Leicester Whirlwind (1759)—This tornado occurred at Leicester, five miles west of Worcester, in central Massachusetts and was described in some detail by Prof. John Winthrop of Harvard. He writes:

> The other account I had in view, is of a whirlwind, which happened on Tuesday, the 10th of this instant July, at Leicester, a town in this province situated about 40 miles west from hence. In point of violence, it seems to have equalled any, and exceeded most, that have happened in this country. At Leicester, several people of credit say, that about five o'clock the sky looked strangely; that clouds from the southwest and northwest seemed to rush together very swiftly, and, immediately upon their meeting, commenced a circular motion; presently after which, a terrible noise was heard.

Winthrop goes on to relate the tremendous damage done by the "whirlwind," the trees torn up by their roots, barns and houses blown apart, the usual. He goes on:

> It is really extraordinary, that, in so sudden and general a devastation, any persons could escape with their lives. And yet the providence of God so ordered it, that but one life was lost. There were, at that time, in the house fourteen persons: Mr. Lynde, his negro man, nine women and children, and three travellers, it being a public-house; of all which, the negro only lost his life. It is supposed, he was in the west chamber. He was found south, a little easterly from the house, about 8 rods, lying across a low wall, and a bed near him, which had been in the west chamber: his back, thighs, and arms were broken, and he soon expired, in extreme misery. His master, supposed to have been in the west lower room, was found nearly in the same direction, about 2 rods distant. He was winding his watch at that time; and the watch was found at one distance, and the case at another. . . . A child, standing near the chimney, was buried in its ruins; but happily preserved by a piece of board, which falling obliquely against the jamb, secured it from the falling stones. . . .

And here, in Winthrop's narrative, we find his questing mind seeking an answer to this swift and violent event. Along with

Franklin's scientific curiosity, Winthrop's interest in mathematics and physics drove him to find out what had caused this thing. He writes:

> I have now given a very circumstantial account of the furious blast; being persuaded that an attention to every particular in effects is generally necessary to a discovery of their cause. It appears to me so difficult to assign a cause adequate to these effects, to show by what means a small body of air could be put into a circular motion, so exceedingly rapid as this must have been, that I dare not venture any conjectures about it. It would be a great satisfaction to me, to know your sentiments, or those of any other learned gentlemen of the Royal Society, upon this article.

The Second Drought (1761-62)—A severe drought during the early and mid-summer of 1761 caused great crop damage. Relief finally came in mid-August, but the drought came again in 1762, when fields and villages burned and public fasts were held. Crops that year were very light and hay cost four times the normal price.

The Southeastern New England Hurricane (1761)—One sure way to cure a drought is to bring on a hurricane, and this one was a dandy. It hit on October 23-24, and, as usual, snuck up on the unwary colonists and struck the Massachusetts and Rhode Island coasts very hard. Gale force winds were reported from New York to Maine but the area of the greatest material damage lay in Rhode Island and southeastern Massachusetts. Around Providence "on both roads east and west so far as we have heard, the roofs of houses, tops of barns, and fences have been torn up by the roots by the violence of the storm." Weybosset Bridge across the Head of Narragansett Bay at Providence was wrecked by the wind and tide. At Newport, the steeple of Trinity Church, a favorite target for hurricane winds, crashed to the ground during the blow.

The September Hurricane (1769)—On Friday morning, September 8, a destructive hurricane struck the Carolina coast and roared northeastward, leaving a tremendous path of damage in its wake. Williamsburg, the colonial capital of Virginia, and the towns along

Chesapeake Bay were particularly hard hit, with local flooding, downed trees, and numerous shipwrecks. Further north in Philadelphia and New York, there was similar damage with a widespread report of heavy damage to crops. The storm roared along the New England coast, being felt as a strong northeast gale. On the Harvard campus in Boston, John Winthrop's barometer dropped to 29.57'' during "a great storm of wind and rain," and his rain gage collected a total of 3.7'' during the storm.

The Late Season Storm (1770)—A late season storm in October 1770 struck the New England coast from eastern Connecticut to Maine and achieved lasting renown by bringing in a tremendous tide, said to be the highest since the much-publicized Boston Harbor flood of 1723.

The *New London Gazette* reported a northeast storm on Friday night the 19th which continued into Saturday and drove two vessels on shore. Farther east at Newport, Ezra Stiles, an avid storm-watcher, described the blow on the 20th as "a violent hurricane. Wind N or NE. Rain violent—hail—vane of church steeple blown off." Stiles's thermometer dropped to 35.5° by 7 p.m. and a stiff west wind was blowing. The mention of hail (probably actually ice pellets or sleet) would indicate that a very cold air mass lay to the west of the storm track over western and northern New England, a situation that would certainly intensify the storm circulation.

The Boston area lay within the track of high winds. "Last Saturday morning," reported the *Massachusetts Gazette,* "a most violent storm came on the wind about NNE, attended with rain and hail. The tide rose about noon to such a height that it overflowed most of the wharves in this town. . .it is said that the tide rose higher than has ever been known, excepting once about 47 years ago, it rose a foot higher."

At Harvard, John Winthrop noted an extremely low barometer of 28.96 inches at 3 p.m. on the 20th. "A great storm does a vast damage," he wrote. Rain and hail continued into the evening for a total precipitation figure of 2.48 inches.

The storm area extended northward and northeastward. At Portsmouth several buildings were blown down along with many fences. Here, too, a high tide did much damage to wharves and goods. Inland at Bedford, near Manchester, Matthew Patton noted a very great storm of rain and hail from the northeast that "worked backward to the north." It rained 24 hours steadily there. And at Portland, Rev. Thomas Smith thought it "an exceeding great N.E. storm."

A Remarkable Hurricane (1773)—One or more tornadoes struck the Merrimack River valley in Massachusetts on August 14, 1773, causing tremendous destruction, but no loss of life. Rev. Samuel Williams in a report to the American Philosophical Society, described what happened:

> There was a remarkable Hurricane this year, the effects of which were principally felt at Salisbury, Amesbury, and Haverhill. . . . Its rise was very sudden, and without any previous uncommon appearance in the sky, or other symptom of its approach. In the morning there was a light breeze of wind at the east, attended with plentiful showers. At 7h 3/4 the wind verred about to south-east, where it became a brisk gale. In about two minutes, it got into the south-west, and became on a sudden very violent. From whence in about two minutes more, it shifted to west-north-west, and then suddenly died away to a moderate breeze. While the wind was thus changing, it

seemed to blow in every direction; the gusts became very violent, and formed many little whirlwinds all around, attended with a very heavy shower of rain, and an uncommon darkness. . . . Several buildings were shattered to pieces, and others removed in an instant. A sailmaker's loft in which a man was sitting, was carried away and dispersed in a moment; the unhappy man being found senseless at a distance of 94 feet from the place where the loft stood. A large oak post 14 feet in length and 11 inches in diameter, was taken up and carried by the wind 138 feet. Two new vessels of 90 tons burthen, were lifted up from the blocks and carried to the distance of 22 feet. And a large bundle of shingles was taken up from the earth and thrown near 330 feet, in a direction contrary to that of the posts and vessels. The trees around were torn up, the fences were thrown down, scattered or carried off, and the various kinds of lumber that lay dispersed on the shore, were whirled about in different directions, and to different distances. Some houses and vessels that seemed the most exposed to the wind, suffered nothing at all; and others that seemed to be the least exposed were much damaged or carried off.

The area of greatest damage was a strip three miles long and one-half mile wide, but downed trees and crop losses were reported up to eight miles on each side of the tornado's path.

The Independence Hurricane (1775)—A savage hurricane swept out of the tropics in September, 1775, just as the opening maneuvers of the War of Independence were in progress. Smashing over settlements ashore and overwhelming ships at sea, the storm raged from North Carolina to Newfoundland, exacting a toll of human lives higher than any previous mainland hurricane.

In North Carolina, more than 150 lives were lost, mostly due to sinking ships. A Williamsburg, Virginia, paper noted: "the shocking accounts of damage done by the rains last week are numerous; most of the mill dams are broke, the corn laid almost level with the ground, and fodder destroyed; many ships and others drove ashore and damaged at Norfolk, Hampton, and York." At Philadelphia, Phineas Pemberton noted:

> Sept 3— Stormy & showery. A violent gale from NE to SE the preceding night with heavy rain, lightning and thunder—a remarkably high tide in the Delaware this morning. Flying clouds & wind with sunshine at times P.M.

New England lay well to the east of the central track of the storm, though high winds and heavy rain were reported along the entire coast, disrupting most activities.

Shortly afterwards another storm was reported to have struck Newfoundland with unprecedented force. A traveler from Halifax related to the Boston press that the blow occurred on September 9, a full six days after the above hurricane passed through New England. It is possible that the Newfoundland storm could have been the same, but it is also quite logical to believe that it was a second storm. The Newfoundland blow caught many fishing boats on the Banks and drove them ashore before they could seek shelter in harbors. Four thousand sailors were reported to have drowned, most of them from Irish and English fishing ports. On land, roofs were torn off, chimneys crumbled, and houses collapsed from the force of the wind.

The Ordering of Providence (1778)—A hurricane of moderate size moved along the familiar tropical storm track close to the Georgia and South Carolina coasts on the 10th and 11th of August, 1778. A French fleet was rapidly closing on the British under Howe in the late afternoon when the first puffs of a hurricane approaching from the south began to kick up the seas. In view of the lateness of the hour and the increasing storm, the French bore away to the south and by sundown all were under close-reefed topsails.

> The wind now increased to great violence, and a severe storm raged on the coast until evening of the 13th, throwing the two fleets into confusion, scattering the ships, and causing numerous disasters. The *Apollo* lost her foremast, and sprung the mainmast, on the night of the 12th. The next day only two British ships of the line and three smaller vessels were in sight of their Admiral. . . . Many injuries had been received by the various ships, but they were mostly of a minor character; and on the 22nd the fleet again put out to sea in search of the enemy.

The French had suffered much more severely. The flagship *Languedoc* had carried away her bowsprit, all her lower masts followed it overboard, and her tiller also was broken, rendering the rudder unserviceable. The *Marseillais* lost her foremast and bowsprit. In the dispersal of the two fleets that followed the gale, each of these crippled vessels, on the evening of the 13th, encountered singly a British 50-gun ship; the *Languedoc* being attacked by the *Renown*, and the *Marseillais* by the *Preston*. The conditions in each instance were distinctly favorable to the smaller combatant; but both unfortunately with-drew after nightfall, making the mistake of postponing to tomorrow a chance which they had no certainty would exist after today. When morning dawned, other French ships appeared and the opportunity passed away.

Ashore at Newport the hurricane gave the land troops a severe beating. Lt. Frederick MacKenzie of the Royal Engineers was at hand to record the military happenings along with perceptive meteorological comments:

> 13 August—The rain continued very heavy from 4 o'clock yesterday evening, all last night, and all this day; with a very strong gale of wind at N.E. The wind fell about 8 this evening. Most of the tents are blown down and torn to pieces; particularly those constructed by the Seamen of the ship's sails. Much damage is done to the Indian corn, a great part of which is laid quite flat. The troops are at present in a most uncomfortable situation, few of the officers having a tent standing, and every thing belonging to the men being perfectly soaked with the rain. We are under great apprehension for the safety of Lord Howe's fleet. . . .

On the night of the 11th and throughout the 12th and 13th the hurricane was felt up and down the Middle Atlantic and New England shores as there were gale reports from Boston, Salem, and Dover in New Hampshire. But it appears that the worst of the blow remained offshore since all wind reports are northeast. The greatest reported damage occurred on the two opposing fleets which must have been rather close to the center of this northeastward-moving hurricane.

Famous Dark Day (1780)—On May 19, 1780, New Englanders became increasingly frightened as mid-day darkness spread southward from Vermont to Cape Cod. The landscape took on a grey to yellowish-green hue and the churches filled as the populace thought the end of the world was at hand. The cause: smoke from tremendous forest fires to the west.

The Tornado Outbreak (1782)—The sparsely settled area of northwestern Massachusetts, southern Vermont, and the middle Connecticut Valley of New Hampshire was hit by a swarm of tornadoes on Sunday afternoon, May 23, 1782. There seemed to have been two main veins of tornado activity, though it is impossible to determine whether a skipping action was present. The trend of the veins appears to have been from southwest to northeast. Thus, a track might have led from western Vermont over the mountains to eastern Vermont. Another might have originated in Berkshire County and crossed into Vermont. To the northeast of these, tornado damage was reported in the Wethersfield-Claremont area on the Connecticut River. Most probably, other tornado tracks that afternoon went entirely unnoticed or unreported.

Typical of the reports is this one which appeared in the *Connecticut Courant*:

> The amazing horrors of yesterday afternoon, almost
> surpass belief, and baffle all my powers of description.

About three o'clock in the afternoon, the wind about N.W. blew a most terrible hurricane; Many trees were torn up by the roots, others twisted off and carried by the violence of the gale to an incredible distance and while fields of grain were swept entirely away. It ran in a vein about half a mile in width, and produced as great a scene of devastation and horror in its course, as perhaps was ever exhibited in this part of the world. Every house, barn, or building of any kind which stood in its range was raised to the foundation or racked or torn in a terrible manner. Mr. Spencer's house was blown down, the very cells were torn up and twisted like a withe. Mr. Spencer caught his little daughter, a child of ten years of age in his arms, and attempted to make his escape with her, when he was buried in the ruins of his house together with his wife, and the child killed in his arms; Mr. Spencer and his wife were dug out of the ruins soon after the storm abated, he escaped himself with very little hurt, his wife was terribly wounded but it is hoped she will recover.

The Stormy October (1783)—In October, 1783, two major storms, both conceivably of tropical origin, swept up the Atlantic seaboard, bringing destructive gales, heavy precipitation (some of which fell as snow over the northern interior), and destructive floods when a third rainstorm caused a rapid snow melt and runoff.

The first disturbance seems to have been an authentic hurricane. On October 7th, it hit Charleston, S.C., a severe blow and moved up the coast with exceedingly high winds and rain to smack Richmond, Norfolk, Philadelphia, and New York where there was "an uncommon high tide attended with a hard gale," flooding cellars along the waterfront and overflowing wharves. New Haven, Providence and Boston all reported gale force winds and dangerous tides.

A second storm, packing winds of less violence but producing a greater precipitation output, moved up the coast on the weekend of the 18–19th. A good reservoir of cold air lay over Canada. This contributed to a considerable deepening of the storm center off the New England coast and brought a mid-October snowfall almost to the shores of Long Island Sound.

Back in the hills of Vermont, the snowfall reached a depth of 6 to 8 inches on the height-of-land to provide a good runoff on a soil already saturated from a wet September and the early October hurricane. Another heavy rainstorm struck the Vermont area on Wednesday, the 22nd, as reported in the Windsor *Vermont Journal*, "which raised streams to such a degree as produced the greatest flood ever known since the settlement of this country." Bridges and mills were washed out, and traveling was reported to be extremely difficult.

Tornadoes on the Housatonic (1784)—Central Connecticut was hit by several tornadoes on August 17, 1784, causing the usual "producing such a scene of desolation as perhaps the memory of the oldest men cannot recollect to have been produced by a similar cause" comments. The areas affected were on a southwest-northeast line running from South Britain to Southington. Again, the usual houses were blown down, orchards destroyed, children "carried a dozen rods" through the air with minor injuries, and the funnels were attended by "the most tremendous thunder and lightning."

One reason that the violence and destruction of tornadoes will probably always be described by witnesses as "the most horrible thing ever known in the memory of the oldest person" is because they are so localized and happen so quickly. Areas affected by tornadoes are usually less than two miles by one-half mile, and consequently there are not many people who have experienced them more than once in a lifetime, especially in the Northeast. Remember the amazement of the people of Hartford when they learned that the Windsor region (a few miles to the north) had been blown to smithereens by a tornado in the summer of 1979? They couldn't believe it; all they had from the same storm were a few thundershowers.

The Equinoctial Storm (1785)—A heavy gale swept the eastern seaboard on September 23–24, 1785, shortly after the equinox. In the Carolinas and Virginia, there was severe inland flooding with the loss of many cattle and much damage to ships. Further north, Baltimore, Philadelphia, New York and Boston all reported high winds, flooding and heavy damage.

More Tornadoes in Connecticut (1786)—The northeast Connecticut towns of Woodstock, Pomfret and Killingly were struck by a tornado on August 23, 1786. Lightning was a factor in this storm with reports of fires being started, cows killed, and at least one person struck by a bolt. Destruction from the winds was severe, but perhaps the most interesting report of the storm (for modern comparison purposes) comes from a story which appeared in the *U.S. Chronicle* in Providence:

> The following is an account of the damage sustained by the inhabitants in the tornado on the 23rd of August last, viz.— Dwelling houses damaged, 20 — Barnes and outhouses destroyed and damaged, 63 — Apple trees destroyed, 2478; other fruit trees not numbered. Acres of woodland destroyed and damaged, 1000 — Stone-walls, other fences, English grain, standing corn, pulse, hay wool, flax, household furniture, and lumber destroyed and damaged, the whole damage amounting to £1,791.

It's incredible to realize in our age of inflation and unrealistic prices that all that loss to property, land, and crops adds up to less than $10,000. By today's standards, a similar loss would probably go into the tens of millions. Ah, for the good old days.

Triple Big Snows (1786)—There had been no really tremendous snowfalls in the Northeast since 1717, but in December, 1786, the snow, so to speak, hit the fan. The Triple Storms, occurring on December 4–5, December 7–8, and December 9–10, were back-to-back, allowing no time for thaw or clearing. In New Haven, the total accumulation was 37 inches. Farther north, Boston recorded four feet on the ground. Unfortunately, the third storm was accompanied by high winds and great tides, destroying wharves and shipping. To compound the troubles, the Triple Storms were followed on December 12th by a record early cold wave (12° below at Hartford).

The Four-State Tornado Swarm (1787)—Tornadoes are relatively uncommon in the Northeast, but that fact could not be proved by the latter part of the seventeenth century. In mid-August, 1787, commencing in central Connecticut, a series of tornadoes touched down in Rhode Island and Massachusetts; they ended in southern New Hampshire and represented the most extensive tornado outbreak in early New England. Only the tornado activity on September 9, 1821 in the central and upper Connecticut Valley could equal this event for widespread atmospheric turbulence in New England. The first tornado took place between one and two o'clock on August 15, 1787 at

New Britain, south-southwest of Hartford. Wethersfield immediately to the northeast was next.

The spread of damage extended on the west from Rutland in western Worcester County, Massachusetts to Gloucester in northwestern Rhode Island on the east. The northernmost touch-down occurred at Concord, New Hampshire, and at Rochester, close to the New Hampshire-Maine border. But these places lie northeastward from Rutland and Gloucester. Thus, the area of northeast-moving turbulent activity extended over a rectangular area about 30 miles wide and about 145 miles long.

Much devastation occurred in east-central Massachusetts, close to the center line of the tornado swath, north-easterly from Wethersfield. This was the area struck by the last stages of the Great Worcester County Tornado in 1953, but on this occasion the storm system originated to the northwest and swept eastward through this area. No large cluster of buildings or village was struck by the 1787 funnels, so damage was at a minimum and few lives were lost, but the physical potential was there.

George Washington's Hurricane (1788)—An early season hurricane of great destructive power caused many ship disasters as it swept the ocean area south and west of Bermuda in late July, 1788. It then roared inland on a northwesterly course over tidewater North Carolina and Virginia.

George Washington, at Mt. Vernon, some 140 miles northwest of Norfolk, noticed a quick shift in wind from northeast and south. Washington's diary usually paid great heed to the current weather situations and the present storm received full attention:

> Thursday - July 24th. Thermometer at 70 in the morning, 71 at noon, and 74 at night. A very high No. Et. wind at night, which, this morning, being accompanied with rain, became a hurricane, driving the miniature ship *Federalist* from her moorings, and sinking her, blowing down some trees in the groves and about the houses, loosening the roots, and forcing many others to yield, and dismantling most, in a greater or lesser degree of their bows and doing other and great mischief to the grain, grass, etca. and not a little to my mill race. In a word it was violent and severe -

more than has happened for many years. About noon the wind suddenly shifted from No. Et. to So. Wt. and blew the remaining part of the day as violently from that quarter. The tide this time rose near or quite 4 feet higher than it was ever known to do, driving boats, etc. into fields where no tide had ever been heard of before, and must, it is apprehended, have done infinite damage on their wharves at Alexandria, Norfolk, Baltimore, etc. At home all day.

The *Maryland Gazette* at Annapolis noted the greatest tide in memory with northeast winds which gradually veered to southeast, but no abrupt shift to southerly took place, to put the Maryland capital east of the track of the center. At Baltimore a violent storm from the east-northeast raged for 12 hours.

The Alexandria reports confirmed Washington's account of the sudden wind shift:

Alexandria, 31 July. The wind was ENE when the storm began, but changed suddenly to the southward and brought in the highest tide that was ever known in this river. The damage in the country to the wheat, growing tobacco, Indian corn, &c. is beyond description; and many planters and farmers, who flattered themselves with much greater crops than have been known for many years past, had their hopes blasted by the violence of the storm.

There are no further notices of the hurricane from any location north of Maryland and Virginia. It is assumed that the momentum of the whirl kept it moving northeastward into the Appalachian Mountains of present West Virginia, Maryland and Pennsylvania.

Hurricane, Tornado or Squall Line? (1788)—From the scientific point-of-view the most fascinating of all the severe storms studied in this period occurred in mid-August 1788, just a month after George Washington's Hurricane had swept inland over North Carolina and Virginia with devastating effect. The August storm of 1788 appears unique, without known precedent.

A tropical hurricane lashed Martinique in the Windward Islands on August 14th, the gale commencing in the morning at northeast and continuing until about 11 pm between northeast and north-northwest. At that time there was a sudden shift to southwest with redoubled violence, a wind maneuver which appears again and again in the later history of this storm. Puerto Rico and Haiti were visited by a severe storm two days later, on the 16th, and 50 vessels were reported driven ashore. It would appear that these two were the same storm.

The next land report comes from Philadelphia where on the 18–19th a tremendous downpour of tropical proportions deluged the city as a preliminary to a severe wind storm which swept over New Jersey, New York, and New England during the daylight hours of the 19th.

What's interesting about this particular storm is that, in the true sense, it is hard to class this storm as a hurricane. The path of destruction, tracking from Morristown, New Jersey, up the Hudson River Valley and across Connecticut to western Massachusetts and Vermont was only about 50 miles wide and the duration of the heaviest part of the storm was a mere thirty minutes or less.

The question arises as to what this storm was. Hurricane? Tornado? Line Squall? First of all, a fair estimate of its forward speed can be made. The airline distance from New York City to Northhampton, Mass, is about 130 miles and the center apparently took about three hours, if one can depend on the press figures, to make the journey at a rate of about 45 mph. This forward progression of the storm over New England from southwest to northeast and the fact that the severe part of the blow came from different directions at different places would rule out the possibility that this was merely a line squall. Further, the great amount of rainfall accompanying the western section of the track rules out the line-squall hypothesis.

The forward rate of 45 mph would not be unusual for a well developed tornado, but nowhere was the rotary wind movement characteristic of a tornado. The wind at any single location was always reported as coming from a single direction.

Therefore, the assumption that this was a true hurricane must be correct and directly related to the tempest which moved through the eastern West Indies on August 14–16. It is probable that this tightly-knit storm of very small diameter made no landfall before the Delaware Bay area. No ship reports of damage at this time have been noted, and no mention appeared in the Norfolk or eastern Carolina papers.

The wind action is certainly like no other hurricane which has ever affected this area. The extremely short period of severe wind force, estimated from 15 to 25 minutes at several points, would indicate a very small center, and also a rather fast forward movement. It is probable that the area of high winds did not exceed 100 miles in breadth, but in about a fifty-mile-wide path the speeds must have been well in excess of 75 mph to cause such destruction, especially in the forests. One can contemplate the damage a repetition of such a powerful storm would cause in this now heavily-populated strip from New Jersey to interior Maine.

The Most Tremendous Tornado (1794)—Late in the day on June 19, 1794, a tornadic vein commenced near Poughkeepsie on the Hudson River and ran south-eastward across Connecticut with extensive damage from New Milford in the western part of the state to Northford in the New Haven area.

While the storm was terribly destructive and violent, a report in the June 24th issue of the *Connecticut Courant* (describing the twister at New Milford) must be placed at the top of the list in the annals of meteorological journalism:

> But those who were near it and just escaped, had a different view still: a view most awfully sublime. It passed like a high and extensive flood of darkness, tumbling and curling with the most rapid motion, in the wildest confusion, full of branches of trees, boards, doors, casks, cloths, wool, and some think they saw animals of various kinds, it is certain, many geese, fowls, &c. are missing where it passed in this town, and cannot be found. One thing

deserves particular notice for its sublimity; it was a Tamarac tree which had been taken up by the roots, and was carried along in the position it grew. Sometimes it would settle down almost to the ground, then rise with rapidity 300 feet in the air: thus it danced along till it went out of the view of the astonished spectators, and what heightened the sublimity, 2 or 3 large objects, supposed to be barn-doors, appeared to play with the tree, attending around it in all its vagaries.

The Ridgebury Tornado (1797)—The tornado that orginated near North Salem, New York, in Westchester County near the Connecticut border on the afternoon of October 8, 1797 cut an unusually wide path. The wind current passed east-southeastward across the Nutmeg State and entered Long Island Sound east of New Haven. The principal destruction occurred in the Ridgefield area south of Danbury in Fairfield County. Then the funnel skipped to East Haven where the next reported structural damage took place. Upper parts of buildings and tops of trees were severely hit. Destruction of the same type occurred at Branford immediately to the east and close to the shore of Long Island Sound.

Among the descriptions of the tornado in the *Connecticut Courant* is the following woeful tale of one Mr. Northrop:

> In the parish of Ridgebury, several houses were demolished, one of which belonged to Mr. James Northrop, caught fire, and consumed, together with all his household furniture, wearing apparel, &c. This unfortunate man, in attempting to escape the fury of the boisterous element, was struck down by a piece of timber and much bruised. Recovering a little, he perceived his daughter lying senseless on the ground, when he raised and conducted her to a place of safety, being both so much bruised as to be incapable of extinguishing the fire that was then kindling in the rubbish of the house. They have since kept to their bed, but hopes are entertained of their recovery. A fine orchard belonging to Mr. Northrop shared the same fate of many orchards, the trees being torn up by their roots and some hurled twenty rods from their former position.

The Bozrah Tornado (1799)—In 1799, the area to the northeast of Norwich in southeastern Connecticut suffered two damaging storms. The towns of Franklin, Lebanon, and Bozrah experienced a devastating hailstorm on July 15th and a small tornado on August 2nd. A committee from these towns appointed to survey the damage issued a report which reads in part:

> One circumstance was extraordinary. The whole destruction by storm, was accomplished almost in an instant. It appeared to be but a single gust of wind, which lasted in no one given space more than a minute. Indeed it was so instantaneously done and the people were in such amazement and terror from the roar of the wind and the danger from their houses, that few if any of them, saw or were sensible of the damage abroad, until afterwards. They saw the trees standing before the storm, and they saw them fallen, after it – it was so sudden they can give no other account of it. . . . A summary of the damages caused by the tornado enumerated: 11 squares of glass – 3 ½ tons of hay – 597 apple trees destroy'd equal to 303 barrels of cider – 3 barns destroyed – 4 ditto unroofed – 1 house destroyed – 1 ditto unroofed – 1 corn house destroyed – 1 shop ditto – 1 shed ditto – Total amount 1315 dollars, 92 cents.

"*Property Damage is Estimated at . . .*" — The Nineteenth and Twentieth Centuries

We have seen that weather disasters during the colonial period provoked widespread misery and suffering. During the final 180 years of our survey, though, the effects of bad weather began to be measured more and more in economic terms instead of physical terms. Nowadays, you almost expect to hear a report like "The devastating damage of Hurricane Bruce on the Gulf Coast will cost 4 billion dollars to repair. Economic emergencies have been declared in four states; the federal government has made low interest loan money available to small businesses; insurance companies have set up field offices; the banks are expected to reopen on Monday. Oh, by the way, 118 people were killed."

Anyway, I will spare you the fine details of these "modern" disasters, and just describe what happened in general terms. I think we've had enough of "Mistress Brown lost her cherry trees." So let us proceed to. . . .

The New England Snow Hurricane (1804)—This was a most unusual early October snowstorm combined with a tropical storm that unfortunately packed hurricane force winds. This misguided system flew up the middle Atlantic states and New England on Tuesday, the 9th of October. At Salem, a Reverend William Bently, who had the dull job of keeping the meteorological records, recounts, "All accounts which I have seen represent nothing like it. In Boston, the old people are said to represent that a storm like it happened on the 16th of September, 1727." Here are a few snow depths: in the Connecticut valley, 15–18 inches fell, and western Massachusetts received 24–30 inches.

The Great Coastal Hurricane (1806)—This lovely outrage of nature descended upon the Atlantic coast on the 21st of August and stayed around until the 24th. As the hurricane gained momentum along the coast, it severely damaged coastal communities and one ship, *Rose In Bloom*, lost 21 persons off Barnegat Inlet on the central Jersey coast. It gave New York City a fine lashing (something it needs plenty of today) and side-swiped Cape Cod, causing great winds and heavy rains. At Edgartown, on Martha's Vineyard, someone noticed that their thirty inch barrel was filled to the brim. Perhaps this islander was filled to the brim instead.

The Cold Friday (1810)—Here is one to put in your cookie jar. Imagine if you will a mild lovely day of gentle breezes with the smell of apple pie in the air, and all of a sudden things change in a classic fit of manic depressiveness to a refrigerative night. A north wind from Canada had crept up on the unsuspecting population lowering the temperature from a balmy 42° in the afternoon to an abysmal 13° below that very evening. Many people were frostbitten on that uncaring day.

The Not-So-Great September Gale (1815)—Who would ever believe that a hurricane could make landfall at Old Saybrook, Connecticut. But strange as it may seem, one did on September 23rd of 1815. It cut New England northward and there was great havoc along the entire coast from New London to points east. Providence was flooded up to its ears and the forests had massive blow downs in eastern Massachusetts, New Hampshire, and Maine.

A Summer Cold (1816)—We have seen how, of late, many people have left New England for the southwest in search of better jobs and cleaner air. Back in 1816, many colonists got "Ohio Fever" when in the early part of June a cold snap and snow made an appearance. This insane condition persisted throughout July and August and fireplaces were lit everywhere because of the frigid nights. To add to the bleak summer there was a drought, and in the fall, a killing frost. As a result of this awful weather, crops failed and man and beast had to tighten their belts. This was also known as the "Year Without a Summer."

The Windy Twins (1821)—I can accept a windy week but to have to repeat the entire affair the following week is just a little too much. On September 3rd a cutie named Redfield's Hurricane stormed ashore at Stamford, Connecticut, and continued unabated to the Berkshires leaving great damage in its wake. On its heels, on September 9th, came the Great New Hampshire Whirlwind, dancing across the Connecticut Valley and into Lake Sunapee, over Mount Kearsarge and into the Merrimack Valley. I understand that for 14 days the people of New Hampshire could not keep their hair combed.

The Cold Shoulder (1835)—Every time a wind blows from Canada in the winter months it makes one wish there was a wall two thousand feet high running the entire length of the northern United States. An Arctic outbreak on December 15–16 ruined many thermometers as the temperature dove to – 20° in the north. In Boston, not only did the temperature reach new lows of – 10°, but the city had to contend with a strong northwest gale.

An Unexpected Thaw (1839)—"I thought I thaw an unexpected thaw," were the words uttered by many frazzled New Englanders when a severe storm rolled over Pennsylvania and New York on January 26–27th. This confused system had the temerity to raise zero temperatures to the mid 50's in the blink of an eyelash, melting the rivers and causing ice jams and extensive flooding. There was also a great rain storm during this madness and there must have been talk of moving back to the mother country.

A Crude Winter Week (1857)—A foot is a foot but a foot of snow is a mile. I can't stand heavy snow. I know it insulates the ground so that the spring flowers can bloom but I fear that the snow has buried more colonists than flowers grew. This northeaster gave New England a foot of snow under zero conditions on January 18–19 and continued with severe cold outbreaks through the 24th. Temperatures ranged from 20° below to an incredible – 45°. This was the coldest January since 1780.

Water, Water Everywhere (1869)—A little flooding is okay if you happen to read about it in the Bible, but when a torrential situation visits your doorstep a feeling of hopelessness pervades your whole being. A hurricane hit eastern Maine and the Bay of Fundy on October 3–4th causing great damage at Eastport; this was combined with what we call a trough to deluge all of New England with a good soaking of six inches of rain. As a result, the greatest six state flooding of the nineteenth century occurred and many drowned. Truly a Biblical situation if I ever heard of one.

A Tornado In Wallingford (1878)—Yes, my fellow weather aficionados, a powerful and cruel tornado stalked through the residential area of northern Wallingford on August 9th. It destroyed a church as well as a colony of Irish immigrants. Thirty-four souls lost their lives and 100 were injured. A vast sum for those days, $200,000, had to be spent for renewal.

The Scorpio Breeze (1878)—Astrologically speaking, October 23rd begins the reign of Scorpio and this central New England hurricane decided to slam into Albany, Concord, and Kennebunkport. It destroyed the only anemometer in Portland, created the highest of tides, ruined the harbor, and reduced the tree population inland.

Cape Cod Hurricane (1879)—As the song says, "You're Sure to Fall in Love with Old Cape Cod," but there wasn't much love at Buzzards Bay in '79 when the barometer read 29.05''. The wind exceeded 50 mph and there was extensive damage on the Islands and Cape Cod.

The Yellow Day (1881)—On September 6, the earth stood still when an enormous smoke screen (emanating from forest fires in Michigan) filtered the sun's rays over New England and created a semidarkness; oil lamps burned in all the villages and towns during the day and a yellowish tinge covered everything including the people who must have thought that the plague was about to destroy them. It was a very hot, still day with temperatures of 90 degrees and above.

Blizzard of 1888, Greatest Storm of the Modern Period—There is nothing like a coastal storm to thrill the heart of many a New Englander and this one stalled near Block Island. On March 12th, a frigid air mass to the west created an unnecessary amount of snow that unfortunately fell for three days and nights in an almost Biblical fashion in Connecticut, Massachusetts, Vermont, and southern New Hampshire. There were 50 inches at Middletown, Connecticut, 46 inches at New Haven, Connecticut, and Albany, New York, 36 inches in Vermont and Cape Cod; unimaginable drifts abounded everywhere and all communities and commerce were halted for a week.

Three Little Words: Hurricane, Hurricane, Hurricane (1888)
—Triplets come in threes, so do knocks on doors and the three little pigs. But for Mother Nature to have the temerity of bestowing upon us the likes of three hurricanes in a row is simply an act of malevolence. Luckily the first of the three, on August 21st, passed well to the east, giving a moderate gale and heavy rain. But on August 24th, the second hurricane took a track from Stamford – Pittsfield – Woodstock – Fort Kent; 300 elms were downed in New Haven, the oyster beds were ruined, and the tobacco crop was almost wrecked in the Connecticut Valley. The third of this mighty troika tracked west and north through Harrisburg – Bennington – Hanover – Caribou. But the wind was the worst aspect of this storm, topping 66 mph.

The Three Day Blow (1888)—This beauty of a late season hurricane centered off Nantucket on November 25th and 26th. Winds at Block Island spun at about 65 mph, and a wave had the audacity to top Minot Light (114 feet in height!) and demolish 15 vessels off the coast of Boston.

Vineyard Sound Waterspout, (1896)—Waterspouts are a rare phenomena in nature but one formed at about one o'clock on August 19th off Cottage City (now known as Oak Bluffs) on Martha's Vineyard. It started about 5 miles offshore and attained a height of 3,600 feet. The diameter of the funnel was estimated to be 720 feet. It was formed three times and its greatest duration was 18 minutes. This unusual sight was viewed by hundreds of vacationers and was well photographed.

The Columbus Day Blow (1896)—Imagine a menacing sky filled up with an ominous assortment of meteorological bad guys and a wind of 60 mph but no rain in sight. This is just what happened on October 12th and 13th off the coast of Block Island. "A day practically without precipitation but with destructive easterly gales, high tides, and an unusually heavy surf on the coast." I bet it was heavy!

The Portland Storm (1898)—In the face of natural disaster, humankind has yet to devise a countermeasure for the safety of its souls. And such a cataclysm occured during the Portland Storm. The barometric pressure was 28.90" and harsh winds of 70 mph over Cape Cod and the Islands caused a great loss of life. New London was buried under 27 inches of snow and the *S.S. Portland* sailed into the teeth of the gale, sinking off Cape Cod with no survivors from a list of 191. The total death count of the storm was estimated at 400.

The Great Atlantic Coast Blizzard (1899)—No life was lost here but it was very messy nonetheless. A severe cold wave lasting from February 8th to 11th was followed by a blizzard that developed on the 12th and continued through the 14th. Twenty-four inches of snow fell on Cape Ann and sixteen inches fell on Boston with a temperature of about 10 degrees during the snow. The total snow depth was raised to 23 inches which broke the all-time record.

The New Jersey Ex-Hurricane (1903)—Put this one in your trivia conversation next time you visit a meteorological convention. On September 16, a hurricane decided to make Atlantic City its first stop. But it soon dissipated, giving southern New England some damage. In New Haven, winds whipped up to almost 50 mph, the highest in 30 years.

Christmas Night Storm (1909)—'Twas the first night of Christmas and all through the house, the dishes were flying and so was the mouse. A northeaster developed off the southern coast and packed loads of energy with winds approaching 72 mph at Hull, Massachusetts. Heavy snow fell inland and many ships were dispatched to the deep.

The Hottest Fourth of July (1911)—New Englanders felt the sting of a tropical heat wave that I'm sure must have been the topic of conversation for the day amongst the older population. It was the first time these temperatures were reached in these old colonies: Vernon, Vermont, 105°; Nashua, New Hampshire, 106°; Bridgton, Maine, 105°; Lawrence, Massachusetts, 106°; Boston, Massachusetts, and Albany, New York, 104°. It all happened on July 4, 1911.

A Most Unusual Day on Martha's Vineyard (1916)—It is most unusual for a tropical storm to make first landfall to the north but this transpired on Martha's Vineyard on July 11, 1916. The barometer on Block Island read 29.37'' with forty mile per hour winds. Excessive rainfall was created as tropical air expanded northward.

Winter of 1917–1918, Severest Winter of the Twentieth Century—It had to happen during the only year the American troops participated in the First World War. It was the coldest December and January on record as a cold wave arrived on Christmas afternoon and decided to remain in our midst until January 4; more of this misery came back on January 18 and held through February 3. The January temperature averaged 9° below normal.

The Great Snow and Sleet Storm of February (1920)—Bostonians had their proper upbringing halted momentarily when a storm so malevolent in its intensity paralyzed the city. From February 5th to the 7th, 12 inches of snow fell, and then to add insult to injury, 3.7 inches of sleet mixed in with some more snow to make it a total of 19.8 inches of misery. It all froze into an icy mess and much of it remained until the end of March.

An Icing In November (1921)—As beautiful as an ice storm can be to the eye, the danger it can create is devastating. Central New England was hit with its most horrid icing experience on November 26th through the 29th. At its worst, the storm left a three inch accumulation of ice on wires and trees. There were electrical outages, little transportation, suspended business, and enormous damage to the forests.

How About an Offshore Hurricane (1924)—The Offshore Hurricane of '24 was centered about fifty miles off Nantucket, Massachusetts. Blue Hill, near Boston, had uproarious winds of 60 mph. There was extensive damage in Rhode Island and Massachusetts and lots of crop damage. And talk about rain—6.36 inches fell at Fall River.

The Vermont Flood of November (1927)—A moist tropical air mass became somewhat confused and traveled up the Atlantic Coast with nothing but malice in its heart. The greatest rainfall occurred in the Green Mountains with the precipitation reaching a total of 9.35 inches. All streams in Vermont, New Hampshire, Westen Massachusetts, and Connecticut were flooded. A total of 84 lives were lost and there was 28 million dollars in damage to Vermont alone.

Tropical Storm Fifteen (1933)—They called it tropical storm 15 because it was the fifteenth of 21 that drenched New Englanders in the year of 1933. It was the most active season in modern times for these moisture laden inventions of Mother Nature. On September 17-18, this storm passed 76 miles southeast of Nantucket with wind speeds of 54 mph. There was 9.92 inches of rain at Provincetown in twenty-four hours, and when it was all over there was a fantastic 13.27 inches of rain on and in the ground. Needless to say, there was general flooding.

New England's Coldest Temperature (1933)—If you decided to celebrate the New Year in 1933 by taking a stroll with your beloved among those frozen woods of long ago, I am sure that the memory of chilly kisses still lingers in the back of your mind. It was on the evening of December 30, 1933, that New England registered the lowest temperature ever with a reading of − 50° recorded by the weather service at Bloomfield on the upper Connecticut River in the northeast kingdom of Vermont.

The Coldest Month on Modern Record (1934)—And in keeping with the frigid nature of this season it would be edifying for me to relate the coldest month on modern record in southern New England. It was February of 1934 and many areas broke all-time minimums. Some examples were: Boston − 18°, Providence − 17°, New Haven − 15°; some state minimums were: Connecticut − 26°. Rhode Island − 22°. Massachusetts − 27°. February of 1934 was the coldest month since January, 1857.

All New England Flood (1936)—Imagine if you will those moments in March just before all of the deep snow melts and fills the eye with rapidly moving streams of water. Sounds good enough, but the snow of March, 1936, was just melting when two heavy rainfalls added to the situation and raised most streams and rivers in a three state area to record stages. The Connecticut River peaked at an all time high of 37.6 feet on March 21. Property damage in Hartford was estimated at more than $100 million.

Storm Number 13 (1936)—A real gully washer passed about 40 miles east of Cape Cod on September 18–19, and the barometer at Nantucket read a devastatingly low 29.27″ with the winds whipping up to about 45 mph. The rain was merciless, with Provincetown getting 7.79 inches, Kingstown 6.46 inches; New Haven got away with a paltry 4.73 inches.

The Great New England Hurricane (1938)—This, of course, was the great and terrible hurricane that inspired books and countless articles in newspapers and magazines. On September 21, this killer snuck up and made landfall near Milford, Connecticut. It continued to move northward to New Haven and Hartford and spun up the Connecticut Valley, finally moving in a northwest fashion across Vermont. The lowest barometric pressure was 28.04″ at Hartford and the devilish winds on Block Island gusted to 82 mph for five minutes; at Blue Hill, an unheard-of gust was registered at 186 mph. The result was almost total coastal destruction and extreme tree blowdown inland. Worst of all, 600 souls lost their lives; property damage was estimated at $306 million.

The Valentine Day Storm (1940)—Not only were many frozen hearts left out in the cold this February day, but I was to be born exactly ten months later in the same year. The snow fell by the bucketfull and 14 inches covered the ground in Boston while a northeast gale peaked at 58 mph creating drifts as high as an elephant's eye. Many hundreds of people were left stranded that evening in downtown Boston after attending an ice show featuring Sonja Henie. It is said the divorce rate in "Bean Town" doubled that year.

The Great Atlantic Hurricane (1944)—The Great Atlantic Hurricane! This weird storm caused untold damage in a fairly small area and in a small amount of time. Striking on September 14, the storm's track of destruction started at Point Judith, Rhode Island, and wound up at South Weymouth, Massachusetts. It traveled 67 miles in 110 minutes. Twenty-six people were killed on land and 300 or more were lost at sea. There was also $100 million in damage.

The Snowiest Winter in Southern New England (1947-1948)—In December of 1947, the snowfall average of 23.2 inches was exactly 290 percent above normal and again in January of the next year the snow rose to the occasion by dumping another twenty-six inches or 240 percent of normal. And why should February escape the onslaught: the snow was 116 percent of normal. Altogether the snowfall for the three months averaged 70.2 inches, and Boston set an all time record by properly suffering under 89.2 inches of the white stuff.

Hurricane Dog Center (1950)—It escapes me why this hurricane was called dog, but it transpired on September 11 and 12. Starting 85 miles east of Nantucket, it curved out on a path south of Nova Scotia. This lovely island was battered and blown by 72 mph gusts of wind, while 4.42 inches of rain fell in 24 hours. Ships were lost at sea and the damage exceeded 2 million dollars.

Great Easterly Gale (1950)—It couldn't have developed over a more brotherly city than Philadelphia, as a deep storm center spun its magic up to New York City and back down to Pennsylvania with a strong easterly flow that affected our beloved New England on November 25–26, Thanksgiving weekend. Some of the wind speeds: Hartford—100 mph, Concord, New Hampshire—110 mph, Putnum, Connecticut—92 mph, and the naughty breeze caused lots of structural damage in these areas. In fact, the carving of turkeys was made most difficult as packs of the roasted wonders were seen flying in formation over New York.

Worcester County Tornado (1953)—Some storms were created for pure horror and this particular tornado is still considered the most powerful and deadly ever to travel our way. On June 9, it cut a diagonal path southeastward through Worcester County, Massachusetts, and slammed into Holden and northeast Worcester with devastating results. Ninety-four people lost their lives, 1,288 were injured and damage ranged near the 53 million dollar mark.

Three Hurricanes (1954)—Some folks like to say that bad things come in threes and certainly these three major monsters had a good time making our existences miserable. The first of these was named Carol. On August 31, as it bisected a region from Saybrook, Connecticut, (this is the birthplace of the now famous publishing firm known as Peregrine Press) to Quebec, Canada, Carol commenced to flood downtown Providence and kill 50 of its inhabitants. The cost in dollars reached an astounding 438 million. Just as the population began to rally, another beauty by the name of Edna (September 11) crossed Cape Cod and the Islands. This killer snuffed out 40 lives and left a tab of $40.5 million in damages. To complete the trilogy, a witch by the name of Hazel brushed New England shortly thereafter, but fortunately only one person was killed and the cost was a paltry $350,000.

Floods of Connie and Diane in August (1955)—Connecticut will long remember the tempestuous rains that caused biblical flooding and terrible death and destruction. Hurricane Connie, descending on August 12 and 13, decided to drench the Connecticut earth with monsoon-like rains. Five days later hurricane Diane stalked the region near Long Island and east to Cape Cod dumping an additional 20 inches on the saturated ground, creating the sort of flooding one could only conjure up in a nightmare. All the rivers in Connecticut, Rhode Island, and Massachusetts were in high flood, but it was Connecticut that suffered the most with the extinguishing of 82 souls and a damage estimate of $800 million.

The Great Northeast Snowstorm of February (1958)—Every New Englander fears the nor'easter because it can mean a blinding blizzard fed by high winds and heavy snow. Such a condition prevailed on the 17th of February with a temperature of 10° below and gale force winds and blowing snow. This classic snowstorm flew like an unguided motorcycle through most of New England and let it be known that it was a snowmaker. The following are representative snow height figures for those who suffer from vertigo: Norfolk, Connecticut, 20 inches; Blue Hill, Massachusetts, 22.2 inches; Cavendish, Vermont, 24.3 inches; Lebanon, New Hampshire, 32.5 inches; and how about 15-foot snowdrifts in Vermont!

Hurricane Donna (1960)—It was on the 12th of September that a very windy hurricane found a home over Long Island and moved shortly thereafter in a northeast fashion toward Rhode Island and Maine. The barometer registered a low of 28.55″, which is the same as if a human being had a blood pressure of ten over five—not exactly a healthy condition. This terrible lady danced northerly in a macabre manner, waltzing by Block Island at 95 mph, leaving three dead in her wake.

A Severe Drought in the Northeast (1961-1966)—During 1980 we found ourselves caught in a scary and severe drought. One seldom thinks of the northeastern part of the United States as being bone-dry, or lacking adequate rainfall. But from time to time this region is hit by a lack of water. The period from 1961 to 1966 was one. It appears that a condition of dryness first appeared in September of 1961 and approached severe proportions by the summer of 1962. The winter rains added a little, but did not help much as the reservoir levels were still low in October, 1963. After another wet winter, the drought returned and by September, 1964, the reservoirs were at the lowest levels yet. By 1965, the rains had come back some (to 59 percent of normal) and aided the beleaguered Northeast. But it wasn't until September and October of 1966 that those everloving rains finally came in above normal and relieved the situation for good.

Three Tropical Storms (1961)—Here are three storms that ran amok during those wonderful days when gasoline was still a quarter a gallon and the only Arabs we knew about were in old Rudolph Valentino movies. Esther put her hooped skirt on 50 miles SSE of Block Island on September 21. The winds reached 83 mph and 8 inches of rain fell in Connecticut and Rhode Island, but this Esther was no fool. She performed a loop with her hoop in a unique clockwise manner: south 300 miles to 36° N, then north along 70° W, passing out over Cape Cod and making a landfall on Rockland, Maine, on September 26—all this and little damage was done. The second storm, Frances, moved NNW along the Gulf of Maine on October 9, then did a double back by traveling NE and passing over southwest Nova Scotia. The third, Gerda, approached within 150 miles of Cape Cod on October 20th but missed the coastline, and there was little damage. It's amazing that these three power-houses didn't cause more destruction.

Alma and Daisy (1962)—The names of these storms have to be among the silliest, and in keeping with their names not much happened. Alma reached a position 50 miles SE of Nantucket on August 29 with winds (get this) at 37 mph. You should have stayed home, Alma. At least Daisy had the temerity to travel toward Maine causing excessive rains: Wakefield, Massachusetts, 14.25 inches, and Portland, Maine, 7.71 inches in 24 hours. That a gal, Daisy.

Year-End Down East Blizzard (1962)—It was no fun when this mean ornery blizzard hit the wonderful state of Maine on December 29–31. Its effects were felt in the rest of New England with heavy snow and a severe wind chill factor. In Maine, a new state record was established for a single storm when Orono received 40 inches in a 24-hour period.

The temperature ranged from zero to 15° below with wind gusts running at about 60 mph. And those beautiful places of the rich, Martha's Vineyard and Nantucket, felt the sting of a 3° below temperature, freezing solid most of the champagne on the islands.

Ginny (1963)—This was the only storm to approach New England waters in that year. It passed 125 miles SE of Cape Cod on October 29. Winds at Nantucket blew to 65 mph, and as it crossed Nova Scotia that evening, it caused 100 mph winds off the Maine coast and 18 inches of snow in the interior. An insane 48 inches fell on Mount Katahdin.

Dora and Gladys (1964)—Little Dora and even smaller Gladys were to have a brief moment of life on September 14 and 23–24 respectively, passing well east of Cape Cod. Nantucket had 42 mph winds and heavy rains fell everywhere.

Big Storm (1969)—Texas may dwarf us with oil wells and fancy cars and women, but I bet they never got a snowstorm that lasted for a hundred hours straight with only a twenty-minute intermission. This horrendous moment occurred from February 24th to the 28th and covered Boston with 26.3 inches (a single storm record, my friends). Here are some of the outstanding snow heights for you trivia buffs: Blue Hill 38.7 inches, Portsmouth 33.8 inches, Pinkham Notch, New Hampshire, 77 inches, Long Falls Dam, Maine, 56 inches. This was one wild winter in our area.

Gerda (1969)—You know I may be light-hearted about these hurricanes, but when one does miss, it is cause for celebration. Gerda is a historic near-miss, and fortunately for us it stayed near Nantucket Lightship, 75 miles SE of Cape Cod, where the wind was clocked at 125 mph with gusts reaching a tremendous 140 mph as the center passed overhead. Luckily, Nantucket wound up with a 40 mph wind with gusts to 58 mph. Try to imagine if the center of this storm happened to pass directly over this precious island. It all happened on September 19.

Month of Record Cold (1970)—I shudder to think of what would happen to our already shrinking paychecks if another cold spell like this happened in these oil swindling times. But in January of 1970, we had the coldest month in over one hundred years. That is, the states of Vermont and New Hampshire did. It was Burlington's all-time coldest month with the average at less than 4°.

Doria's Storm (1971)—There are few men in the world who can say with complete certainty that a celestial event warned them of impending doom. Such was my lot when on the 28th of August, 1971, Connecticut was visited by a tropical storm named Doria at the exact moment that I was being married to a young lady whose name was, oddly enough, Dorie. Adding to the debacle, the church was located in the town of Hazardville, Connecticut. Doria crossed the coast near JFK Airport and the storm track moved across Litchfield, Keene, and Caribou. The final result was very heavy rains and, for me, later, a broken heart.

Agnes and Carrie (1972)—Agnes may have been weakened when she hit land near New York City on a NW track on June 22nd, and although Bridgeport had only 37 mph winds and some moderate rain, the most damaging floods in U.S. history occurred in New York and Pennsylvania. This storm was followed by Carrie, who gingerly passed east of Cape Cod on September 3rd with wind gusts of 100 mph on the Cape and 85 mph at Point Judith. Woods Hole wound up with more than 7 inches of rain. I must add that boat travel to and from Martha's Vineyard and Nantucket was cancelled for the day.

The Maine Blizzard (1975)—From April 2nd to the 5th, the most severe winter storm of the season pummelled all sections of Maine. Blizzard conditions abounded in all areas of the interior and the coastal areas received a mixture of rain, sleet, and snow. Two to four feet of snow fell inland while two to five inches of rain drenched the coastal regions. The winds were clocked at 76 mph at Boothbay and 87 mph at West Harpeswell, along the coast. There were, of course, widespread power outages.

The Drive-In Tropical Storm (1975)—On April 3rd, a coastal storm smashed into the coast of Massachusetts with gusts of 72 mph at the Cape Cod Canal. There was plenty of rain and in the northern Berkshires there was a foot of snow. But the kicker occurred at a place called Marshfield, where a howling 70 mph wind blew over a drive-in movie screen that was just about to show (you guessed it) "Gone With the Wind."

Hurricane Belle (1976)—It isn't bad enough that the human condition has had to put up with Ma Bell and Belle Starr, but on the 10th of August, Hurricane Belle very heavy handedly made herself known in these parts as she moved through southern New England, causing widespread damage to central and western Connecticut. At Bridgeport, the winds reached a severe 81 mph.

A Maine Northeaster (1977)—It was on March 22nd that a snowstorm of hurricane proportions carelessly hit the lovely state of Maine. The winds approached the force of that tropical horror and there was heavy snow. Coastal areas suffered severe damage and there was a rash of long-term power outages.

The Late-Season Snow (1977)—It was May 9th and 10th and the trees were full of the lush foliage so touching and uplifting to New Englanders since they only get to see this sort of thing once a year. A vicious late-season storm hit central New England dumping 8 to 10 inches of snow in Connecticut, where the tobacco nets collapsed and trees were hurt considerably. In Massachusetts, a foot of snow fell, damaging the fruit crop and cutting the power to more than 500,000 homes. It was the first time in 107 years of keeping records that a measurable snow depth was recorded in the Boston area in May. And to continue on with this most unusual set of circumstances, Rhode Island wound up with 8 inches of snow, the most so late in the season in its history of record keeping.

The Most Unforgettable Winter (1978)—How can anyone with any sense of drama forget the winter of 1978! I am sure many of you could include a dozen fascinating incidents that probably happened to you or your family and friends. I will begin this most amazing of weather stories with a series of bad-weather spells that took place before the big granddaddy of all storms transpired.

On January 18, in the northwestern part of Connecticut, a heavy snow started to fall in the middle of the night and caused the Hartford Civic Center roof to collapse due to the weight of the snow. This building, the size of two football fields, was filled with five thousand people only six hours earlier. It wasn't the only building to collapse under this snow, but it was by far the biggest. On the 20th of January, more than a foot of snow fell again in Connecticut, and it was the first time the banks had closed since the 1969 snows. About 75 more buildings collapsed under the weight. In addition, there were 70-mph winds blowing about as the strongest northeaster in decades hit the state. Twenty-four hour snow amount records were broken all over Connecticut. In Massachusetts, the same conditions persisted. A record two feet of snow hit the entire state. Plum Island and Nahant were cut off by high tides and snowdrifts.

In New York State, the second major storm of the month hit with six to twelve inches of snow on the 18th only to be followed by the storm on the 20th where another five inches to a foot fell. In Rhode Island, the powerful coastal storm blanketed the area with 15 to 20 inches of snow and a state of emergency was declared by the governor. But it was on the evening of February 5 that I was forecasting the weather at a local television station in Connecticut. I proceeded to tell my audience that a most ominous set of circumstances was combining that could present us with a historic storm the following day. When I got back to the news room an irate viewer got on the phone explaining to me the fact that the sky was totally clear and the stars were shining and that my alarmist prognostication was a sham and that he would prove it by calling back the next day to tell me so. He never called. It was the morning of February 6th and the workers of the world had not listened with a keen ear to what I had said the night before. It was a lesson we all had to learn together, because I had decided to go to New York for my other weather duties when it happened.

The snow started innocently enough, but when it was over two feet deep it began to be called the "Granddaddy" of them all. Besides the snow, the wind was gusting in excess of 70 mph and the tides were three to four feet above normal. Hundreds of people were evacuated in Norwalk and in Old Saybrook several marinas were destroyed. The blowing snow shut down almost all forms of transportation and for the first time in thirty years the mail did not get through.

My wife, Linda, a pioneering woman if ever I met one, in a fit of gusto, decided she should fetch me upon my return from the city. The trains, somehow, were still running. Ella Grasso had declared an emergency and the roads were closed, but this didn't stop this woman of courage. I was astounded by this smiling blonde, who, with a shovel in her hand saved me from a fate worse than freezing. Our voyage home was another adventure, as many cars were stuck and abandoned.

On the following day I called the news director in New York to tell him I couldn't come in. He intoned, "I don't care if you have to take a dog sled to get into the city. You better be here this afternoon!" Thankfully the North Haven Police drove me by jeep to the New Haven railroad station. But I had to use a dog sled to get from Grand Central Station to the Daily News Building where I work. New York City was almost totally shut down, and was, for once, peacefully quiet. Storms, you see, have their good sides as well as their bad.

Tropical Storm David (1979)—There were eight storms named that year: Ana, Bob, Claudette, David, Elena, Frederic, Gloria and Henri. Five were full-fledged hurricanes: Bob, David, Frederic, Gloria, and Henri. For the first time in ten years, Puerto Rico, the Virgin Islands, and Southeast Florida were seriously threatened by hurricanes. Our friends to the south in Mobile, Alabama, and Pascagoula, Mississippi, had their worst hurricanes of this century. Frederic was the first hurricane to strike Mobile directly since 1926. Feisty Fred brought wind gusts of 145 mph to Dauphin Island, Alabama, along with a twelve-foot storm surge which destroyed much of the gulf shore. But it was

David, with winds in excess of 165 mph, that many say would be the most intense hurricane of this century. This is the fellow that devastated the island of Dominica, killing 56 persons and leaving 60,000 of the estimated 80,000 homeless. David struck the city of Santo Domingo with horrible force and the Dominican Republic sustained a death toll of 1,200 with damage in excess of $1 billion. For us here in the northeast, David made his appearance on September 6. By the time David reached New York and southern New England, he had been demoted to a tropical storm and in passing brought wind gusts of 70 to 80 mph. Boats were blown from their moorings and smashed against sea walls. Trees were dashed to the ground, sometimes hitting homes in the process, and electricity was shut off for over a million people. The rain wasn't what we had expected but the winds were pretty significant and the overall effect of David (tropical storm, indeed!) will have a firm place in our hearts and the weather records. By the time David reached Rhode Island, he was over the hill and the people billed it as the "tired" storm which brought light rainfall to the state.

A Kind of a
Short Course
in Weather

Highs, Lows and Lore

Where does this peculiar New England weather come from, and how does it get to be the way it is? Just imagine our Northeast weather as a large bowl of chef's salad where you have combined and tossed about a dozen types of palatable and unpalatable ingredients. (Hold the anchovies for me!)

Time to introduce the main ingredients. In the northern hemisphere there are four more-or-less permanent weather systems just meandering about waiting for something to push them along. In between events they just hang out, or sleep, or maybe check out some of the TV programs bouncing off the satellites.

The first weather system is the Pacific High, occupying millions of square miles north by northeast of the Hawaiian Islands. When disturbed by upper air jet streams and juicy cyclonic activity, the Pacific High wakes up and gets excited, particularly towards the north. Now the high has acquired all sorts of weather goodies, and it goes from its undisturbed state to an agitated state as upper air currents cause the mass to flow off in a journey that may extend thousands of miles. The location and strength of the northern portion of the Pacific High determines how it will enter North America. It can come in at any latitude, and it can be carrying all of the Pacific storms from Japan to Siberia. (You know Siberia. That's when the maitre d' puts you in the back of the restaurant right next to the restrooms.) So the weather from the Pacific High clears customs in, say, Oregon, and proceeds on its long voyage to Hanover, New Hampshire. Having escorted some nasty ingredients to our shores, the Pacific High goes back to sleeping or TV. It leads an intermittent life.

In the Atlantic Ocean, there is another high, quite a bit smaller, that stretches from the middle Atlantic states to Bermuda and the Azores. It is called the Azores-Bermuda High, although in talking about it in the U.S. we usually skip the Azores part of the name. The Bermuda High, like the Pacific High, is a migratory body, but it is usually off the coast of the Carolinas. It acts as a sort of heat pump to bring up all those hot temperatures from the Gulf of Mexico, and it determines the tracks that storm centers will follow across the eastern United States.

So there you have them: two big-time oceanic high pressure systems that just sort of hang around until something gets them wild and woolly. But wait a minute. If there are highs, there must also be lows out there somewhere just to keep things in balance. Or to keep things stirred up.

The principal troublemaker in our part of the world is the Aleutian Low, which lives in the North Pacific around Siberia and Alaska. Not a real high-rent district, but it seems to suit the Aleutian Low pretty well: frigid air comes down from the Arctic, and mild airstreams sweep up from the tropics. They mingle there, and that makes the Aleutian Low one of the world's great storm factories. Every once in a while part of the low will break off from the main and come sweeping eastward across North America. This minestrone soup of events can be felt eventually in Vermont.

Our final character is the Icelandic Low, which lives well north of the Bermuda High. Sometimes it wanders a bit south of its usual location and lies off Newfoundland, where it acts as a sort of magnet or vacuum sucking storms across New England.

The relative strengths and positions of these four major weather systems are pretty much responsible for everything that happens over New England. Depending on whether the Pacific High or the Aleutian Low is predominant in the West, weather foul or fair can start across the country. The Bermuda High and the Icelandic Low will determine how that weather leaves our shores. There are local variations, of course, but these four guys are the Big Picture.

Mankind has probably been hampered in efforts to understand weather because air is invisible, except in New York and Los Angeles. You can watch clouds and see the effects of moisture and air in motion, and deduce the existence of currents, but you can't observe them directly as you can with moving water. But air and water have a lot in common. For example, if you have ever been in an airplane following a 747 or DC-10 too closely, you have learned by getting bumped around a good deal that a 747 leaves a tremendous wake in the air, totally invisible but just as real as the churning water behind The Love Boat. (Pilots sometimes claim that 747's don't really fly —they just push air out of the way.)

The fact that we see and feel the effects rather than the causes of weather had a big effect on our distant ancestors' attitude toward weather and the reasons for it. And it was important stuff: without the rain and the growing season people didn't eat or drink, and we discovered pretty early in our common history that we liked doing those things a whole lot. Our ancestors didn't know about highs and lows, so they created gods. Fair weather and storms depended on the moods of those gods—which isn't so far from our more scientific description of tugs-of-war between lows and highs. We don't offer human sacrifices to appease the Aleutian Low, so to that extent maybe there's been some progress. But along with creating gods, our forefathers put in a lot of time observing weather and its effects on animals and on themselves. And these folk-forecasting methods have survived for centuries.

How many times has Uncle John come up to you and said, "My doggone knees are acting up again and that means rain. And I haven't been wrong in ten years." Of course, Uncle John is a carpet layer, but that never seems to enter into the conversation. He is taking biological clues and basing weather forecasts on them, and this sort of weather-lore predicting has been around a lot longer than that other profession we always talk about in hushed tones. The Egyptians planned their lives around weather lore—remember that the flooding of the Nile was responsible for the creation of an ancient superpower—and the Greeks wrote about weather, notably Aristotle in his work "On Meteors." Shakespeare alluded to weather forecasting in his plays, and the Old English epic poem *Beowulf* includes a sun god who must battle the forces of winter and is destroyed in the process. In the Bible, weather lore abounds. In Matthew 16, Jesus says to the Pharisees and Sadducees: "When it is evening, ye say, it will be fair weather: for the sky is red. And in the morning, it will be foul weather today: for the sky is red and lowring. O ye hypocrites, ye can discern the face of the sky; but can ye not discern the signs of the times?"

Any of you who might have the inclination to think that weather is rather a frivolous preoccupation should think again. If a farmer can predict when the first frost will occur, he can maximize his yield. Ocean-going fleets can lose thousands of dollars a day when boats can't unload at a dock because of bad weather. The Normandy invasion in the Second World War could have been a total failure if the meteorologists had been wrong in their predictions. Construction men can't pour concrete when the temperature is below freezing. A clothing store that anticipates an early spring with racks of swimsuits will make more money than a store stuck with too many heavy coats. And on and on it goes. Weather is really an integral part of our existence, and when it comes to predicting this sometimes fickle atmosphere, it is best to be armed both with scientific weapons and folk wisdom.

I would hate to believe that society has totally rejected the mythologies of the past and concentrates solely on the alleged exactness of science. It would be as tragic for a society to build up a technological community capable of giving its population a great deal of comfort, yet not support its emotional and spiritual needs in terms of great music, art, sculpture, humor, and religion, those things that I believe really connect us to the human race. Besides, there is a joy in the enigmatic and in the mystical, and the only ones I know of who revel in its arena are the people of the land: the farmers and the nature lovers, and I must add, a small community of physicists.

It's wonderful to be a little superstitious and in awe of the order of things in the universe and in this manner see the consistency in nature. A great predictability is revealed to those who can investigate with their mind's eye. This may get me into trouble with a few artistic aficionados, but it's like the person who decides to go to Europe and once there runs to the museum in search of the Mona Lisa, and with fixed eyes studies the face for a moment and quickly surmises that the work is quite silly and walks away. This action dismisses totally the world consensus which for centuries has marveled at the painting's ability to tease and trouble us at the same time. The artist had to strive to put into the work a definite idea. We, in order to enjoy its beauty and meaning, just now strive to find the ingredients that make for greatness. And so it would be wise for that abrupt person to continue to go back to the museum each day until the idea is communicated. I somehow suspect that the careful observation of natural things around us potentially has the same wonder and fulfillment.

So the next time someone says to you, "When spiders weave their webs by noon, fine weather is coming soon," don't laugh in half-hearted amusement as you turn to the *New York Times* for the real answer—go out to a field or to your attic and find out for thyself.

The creatures of nature are so well programmed that their every movement is cause for some sort of weather predicting. Here are just a few of the thousands known. Try them out—you may find them to be more accurate than your "dependable" weatherman.

When the barnyard goose walks south to north,
Rain will surely soon break forth.

If when snow is on the ground,
The guinea hens cry, hallow, and caw,
And the turkey moves around,
There shall surely be a thaw.

When eager bites the thirsty flea,
Clouds and rain you sure shall see

When black snails on the road you see,
Then on the morrow rain will be.

When sheep do huddle by tree and bush,
Bad weather is coming with wind and slush.

When spiders' webs in the air do fly,
The spell will soon be very dry.

Swallows fly high: clear blue sky;
Swallows fly low: rain we shall know.

When the donkey blows his horn,
'Tis time to house your hay and corn.

For ants that move their eggs and climb,
Rain is coming any time.

When the cuckoo sings in the sunny sky,
All roads will soon be dry.

When trout refuse bait or fly,
There ever is a storm a'nigh.

When numerous birds their island home forsake,
And to firm land their airy voyage make,
The plowman, watching their ill-omened flight,
Fears for his golden fields a withering blight.

And then, for those of us who don't have access to pigs and donkeys, here's one we can test every morning over breakfast:

When the bubbles in coffee collect in the center of the cup, the weather will be fair; when they form a ring around the edge of the cup, expect rain; if they float separately over the surface, the weather will be changeable.

So turn off that radio! Turn off that television! Don't ever listen to another weatherman—just pour yourself a cup of coffee, and you'll know as much as they do!

That sort of folk wisdom undoubtedly started on the first day that a cave man looked up and saw a cloud, and it kept on through the centuries of duelling weather gods, and even the Greek philosphers attempted to seek natural causes for weather phenomena. And it survives to the present day—thank goodness—as a commonsense, hand-on, eyes-open, with-it backup to the scientific forecasting methods.

Scientific forecasting started with some basic inventions about 400 years ago. As you all know, you can't be scientific without numbers (quantify that, Isaac!), and Galileo, a definite varsity player in several sciences, allowed numbers to be attached to temperature by coming up with the thermometer around 1600. About a half century later, Evangelista Torricelli came up with the barometer, allowing numbers to be attached to atmospheric pressure. After another 100 years, the hygrometer allowed humidity to be measured; and of course weathervanes and gauges of various sorts were improved during these years. By about 1790, all of the basic instruments had been created, and since then, weather forecasting has become a science, eminently suited to confusing the lot of us.

Ropes are more difficult to untwist before bad weather.

The Story of Weather

The study of current, ongoing fluctuation in the earth's atmosphere is known as meteorology; therefore, the scientist or television forecaster who forecasts storms and droughts is called a meteorologist. Well, not really. The television personality is known as a weatherman or weatherperson or weathergirl or weatherwoman, or just plain entertainer. Fitting into a couple of the aforementioned categories, I will take it upon myself to attempt to explain weather to you perhaps in a way that will delight some and offend others. Whatever—here goes.

I am sure you have had the occasion of walking into a party and exclaiming to your partner, "I don't like the atmosphere," and after gazing in consternation at the group of partygoers, you finally make the great judgment, "Let's get out of here." There was something in the air that was unpalatable to your reason or taste that makes you decide that a speedy exit is the only recourse. Well, the earth also has an atmosphere, and whether you like it or not, the best place for you to be is here, because once you leave *this* party there's only oxygen strangulation and oblivion.

The atmosphere is approximately one hundred miles in depth, and we members of the family homo habilis are residents of the lowest part of this vast ocean, an ocean which is in constant turmoil. As you know, the higher up you go, the thinner the air, and the lower you go the thicker the plot. As a matter of fact, half the weight of the atmosphere is contained in the lowest three and a half miles, and something interesting is going on all the time in this region, including the effects that we recognize as weather. Now you must understand that weather is the topic of conversation in all lands at all times of the day and night. But we in the United States have had the misfortune of having to listen to the weather on the radio one hundred times a day and at least twenty times a day on television, so we get tired of talking about weather. Which leads us to talk about other things like urban crisis, prostitution, and gun control—areas of discussion that will never be resolved anyway. It is my strong belief that they should get rid of weather reports on radio and television. This in turn would be the catalyst for the population to resume the great weather dialogue and in so doing refrain from talking about E.R.A., abortion, and post-menopausal zest. This would return the nation to sanity, and in one stroke we would get rid of the Congress, the Board of Education, the American Medical Association, Dr. Joyce Brothers, William F. Buckley, the Food and Drug Administration, and Ivy League schools. The United Nations would be renamed in honor of America's finest weather man, *The Doctor Frank Field Institute of Weather.* Here, peoples of all nations would talk about how nice and sunny it is today and invite their adversaries to go fishing in the East River and maybe afterwards they would go to Central Park and watch the clouds.

Temperature

How many times have you heard the expression, "she is as cold as a fish?" Well, how cold is a fish anyway? The hotness or coldness of any given fish is called its temperature, a thing that can be measured with a thermometer. A human being has a normal temperature that is equivalent to Eubie Blake's age, 98.6°. A thermometer is a glass bulb attached to a rather thin stem, resembling a high fashion model, with a bore of threadlike diameter. The bore contains mercury, which expands when the temperature rises and contracts when it descends. Obviously, you can see the effect by the height of the column of mercury in the stem. A scale of degrees can be carved on the stem for reading and, in keeping with the accuracy that weather people must maintain, a "real" thermometer is usually hidden in a box resembling a dog house with side vents that allow the air to pass freely around the thermometer but keeps the sun away. Another type of thermometer is a whirling thermometer mounted within a wooden frame that swivels on a handle. Many meteorologists like to bring these instruments to New Year's Eve parties and at twelve o'clock spin them above their heads in gay abandon. There is also the thermograph, an insidious device that records the temperature throughout the entire day. Imagine two strips of different metals fused in a coiled band (just like the ordinary home thermostat) where

If bats cry a lot, it will rain.

there is an uneven expansion of the coil. (The metals expand at different rates when heated.) The differential is then recorded on a graph.

Temperature can be expressed as Fahrenheit or centigrade. As usual, the Americans gave in to the international community and the name centigrade has been replaced by celsius in official U.S. meteorology. For all intents and purposes, the scales are about equivalent except that I find that the Fahrenheit scale is about twice as accurate as the celsius in certain situations. For example, on a given winter night when the temperature is hovering at about 33 or 32 degrees and the difference of one degree is essential to accurately predict snow or rain, the celsius scale would still read zero, which doesn't tell me much about fine gradations. So the celsius scale is very much like a car's speedometer that reads ten, twenty, or thirty miles per hour, but somehow doesn't make sense unless it can also read eleven miles per hour as well.

As you know, there is a freezing point and a boiling point for water, and the centigrade (or celsius) scale divides the range between these two points into one hundred equal parts or degrees; the numbers 0 °C and 100 °C represent the freezing and boiling points, respectively. The temperatures below freezing are represented by a negative number. On the Fahrenheit scale, 32 degrees is the freezing point of water and 212 degrees is the boiling point. A Fahrenheit degree is about one half (actually 5/9) of a centigrade degree. There is also a wonderful scientific scale known as the Kelvin (K) scale which expresses absolute zero, the lowest temperature attainable in the universe. This zero of zeros is revealed as 0 °K; -273.2 °C; -495.7 °F. Hard as it is to believe, my companeros, but all atomic motion ceases at this temperature. 0 °K is pretty damn cold.

When pigs squeal in winter, there will be a blizzard.

Pressure

We all know that the world is full of pressure. All you have to do is get a job or go to school to know that pressure is exerted on all of us to a certain degree. A guy named Torricelli not only noticed his own daily pressure (you can't go around in the world with a name like Evangelista without getting into a fight every time you walk past the Fontana de Trevi in Rome), but he carried out an experiment in 1643 that showed that the atmosphere also exerted pressure on all of us. Torricelli took a straight, narrow tube closed at one end, and put a mess of mercury in it. Then he stood it straight up with its open end sunk in a bowl of more mercury. Some of the mercury in the tube flowed back into the dish, but about thirty inches of mercury remained standing in the tube. What to do? He realized that this could only happen if the atmosphere were pressing on the surface of the mercury in the dish and was supporting the weight of the column in the tube. He also realized that pressure must be evenly distributed over a surface. You all know that atmospheric pressure is expressed in pounds per square inch and at the earth's surface the normal air pressure is about 14 pounds per square inch. But it's interesting to note that the weight of a one square foot column of air extending from sea level to the outer extremes of the atmosphere weighs nearly one ton. Think about that! By the way, atmospheric pressure is usually measured with a mercury barometer, the contraption discovered by Torricelli.

Humidity

"It's not the heat, it's the humidity," How many times have you had this polite conversation with your stockbroker? There is always a little water in the form of an invisible vapor in the air all over the atmosphere. When this vapor condenses, weather is created. That's right, my friends. Rain, clouds, snow, dew, hail, frost and fog are all part of this wonderful process and to understand weather you have got to understand humidity.

If the cock crows going to bed, he will certainly rise with a watery head.

The amount of water vapor in the air is expressed as weight in a specified volume of air; this is expressed in grams per cubic meter. There is just so much water that a given volume of air can hold, and when the volume contains this maximum amount, the air is said to be saturated. Did you know that warm air can hold more water vapor than cold air? For each rise of one degree in temperature, there is a certain increase in the saturation weight. The air is really quite dry most of the time, that is, it contains only a portion of the saturation amount. This portion is known as a fraction and is expressed as a percentage—we all know it as "relative humidity." (Which reminds me of the old saying that states that everything is relative: the more money you have the more relatives you have.) For example, air at 50 °F, if saturated, contains 9.4 grams per cubic meter of water and the relative humidity is 100%. When the humidity is low, the air feels uplifting and your I.Q. actually goes up. When the humidity is high, the air feels moist and heavy and your I.Q. is reduced and you may be rendered helpless and sent by helicopter to the home for the bewildered. Okay, what is all this jazz about dew point? This is when you get in the car in the morning and your warm moist breath creates mist on the car window. Simply stated, the mist on the car window occurs because the temperature of the glass is lower than the dew point of the warm air inside the automobile.

The Atmosphere

Let's take a quick look at the atmosphere. As everyone knows, our air is made up of a constant proportion of gases with nitrogen (at 78%) and oxygen (at 21%) being the most common. The atmosphere is considered to consist of three layers. The lowest, the troposphere, is about five miles thick at the poles and ten miles thick at the equator, and is interesting to us because this is where all the weather action takes place. This is why scientists called this region "troposphere" from the Greek "sphere of change." The area immediately above the troposphere, about six miles thick, is called the tropopause: "where change stops."

When a storm is approaching, sea birds will fly in the air, rarely resting.

The next layer of the atmosphere is called the stratosphere and is about fifty miles thick. Not much happens here. Beyond that there is the ionosphere, about 500 miles thick. *Nothing,* from a weather standpoint, happens here at all. At eleven miles above the earth near the top of the tropopause, we encounter another wonderfully confusing area. From here on up, the temperature remains steady for about twenty miles and then, presto chango, it starts to warm up again. There are no clouds in this quiet place made up of layers of helium and hydrogen, hence the name stratosphere "sphere of layers." Clever, these scientists. Now here is the kicker. As we continue to our dizzying heights, the next section is known as the mesosphere; here the temperature drops once again but then rises up from the ionosphere into the greatest place of all—the boundary with space called the exosphere. If all of this seems confusing, it's because it is, I think. Please don't write me about it. You can get good information in any encyclopedia; I might confuse you further, and we're interested in the lowest layer anyway.

Roberto Tirado's

Temperature and Altitude

Did you know that here on earth the temperature lowers as you gain altitude? The rate of change is about 4 °F per thousand feet, depending on how dry or moist the air is. So if you climb Mount Washington in New Hampshire, all things being equal, it will be about 20 °F cooler than at sea level. This is why when you're flying at 33,000 feet on a steaming hot day, it is somewhat surprising to hear the pilot announce that the outside air temperature is, say, 20° below. Now what is this about unstable air and stable air? Air is constantly circulating (called convection currents). This phenomenon is

When sheep go to the hills and scatter, expect nice weather.

similar to a pot of water boiling on the old stove. The earth absorbs the sun's energy and then reradiates it as heat. Think of the earth as a can of sterno you have lit up under the hors d'oeuvres; the surrounding air is warmed up nicely with the greatest effect near the surface. Now when the air is heated, it expands and becomes less dense and therefore lighter in weight. Voila, it rises, but as it does, it cools off. (They call this the process of adiabatic expansion.) As air expands it loses temperature at a lapse rate determined by its moisture content.

Let's look closer at this exciting process and see how clouds are formed. If you find it a little mysterious, so do I. You go out into the world and look at your outdoor thermometer and it reads 48 °F and as you look up at the sky, you also know that at about one thousand feet the temperature is about 44 °F. But if you are out in the desert and there is dry air at 51 °F (which is warmer than the surface air) then it is going to rise. Dry air rises at a lapse rate of 5 ½ ° per 1,000 feet. So that at an altitude of 1,000 feet the temperature drops to 45 ½ °, but because the temperature at this altitude is only 44 °F, the air keeps rising. Ridiculous but true. Under these conditions they say that the atmosphere is unstable because once the air starts to rise, it will continue to do so. The air is called stable when a rising current reaches a height where through expansion it becomes colder than the air at that altitude and sinks back to its former position. This is known as the "dry adiabatic lapse rate," but dry moist air also likes to cool through expansion, and when the cooling reaches the dew point, it causes the condensation of vapor into tiny drops of water and releases heat. This release of heat through condensation warms the air. As a result, the temperature falls less rapidly in saturated air than in dry air. And our friends the scientists refer to this as the "saturated adiabatic lapse rate" which in this case is about 3 ½ ° per 1,000 feet. Without confusing you any further, when rising moist air reaches its condensation level, the cooling air becomes a cloud. You look up toward the sky and the air above may be full of molecules of water vapor, and yet, be warm enough for those old molecules to keep bouncing about in gay abandon. These guys are so small that the sky looks clear. Then as the air and the water vapor cool off, the molecules begin to stick to their friends, the dust particles. Very soon the dust and water vapor collect into little clusters and all these silly clusters hang out together and form those ever loving clouds we see and have named cumulus. A cumulus is a cute little cloud with a flat base and a head that resembles a cauliflower. Cumulus forms on the tops of thermals (updrafts that are used by glider pilots to fly to enormous heights). If these thermals continue to rise they eventually form cumulonimbus clouds, the famous thunderhead. Sometimes a discourteous warm layer of air hangs obnoxiously above colder air. This is called a temperature inversion and creates an unusually stable state that blocks off the rise of cooler currents. As you can imagine, all the industrial smoke and the fumes we discard every day have no place to go and they are, in fact, trapped; the result is a smog disaster.

Roberto Tirado's

Wind and Sun

How about the wind. We are at the beach and the sun is shining and the sand is burning the bottoms of our feet and so we run like mad to the water which is much cooler than the sand. In so doing, we either die of shock or are greatly relieved. That cold water has cool air above it and this cooled air rolls in from the water and pushes up the warmer, lighter air near your blanket. This can easily be recognized as that marvelous thing called a sea breeze. And that air continues to travel up and across and down to the water again. This process continues as long as the sun keeps the land warmer than the water. At night, when the beach can be lots of fun and the sun goes to rest, the land cools off much faster than the water. (You mean the water at night is warmer than the land? Yes, my aspiring weather-people.) Then the circle turns in the other direction—the lovely warm air over the water is pushed up by the cooling air rolling out from the land and thus a land breeze is created.

So from this elementary lesson we learn that when the warm air is just a little warmer than the cool air, the breeze is quite mild. But as the difference grows, the wind cycle can become vicious and hor-

When the leaves of trees curl during a South wind, it will rain.

When the peacock loudly bawls,
Soon we'll have both rain and squalls.

ribly indifferent to our health. It is the sun that really causes the wind. Without El Sol the air would not be heated, and the air would not flow. So heat and air make the winds of the world.

In order to specify wind, two things are necessary to know: the wind's direction and speed. Direction is always noted in where the wind is coming from, and the speed is expressed in miles per hour, except when things get hairy. Then they pick up ominous names like gale (38-55 mph), storm (55-74 mph), and hurricane (over 74 mph). The strongest wind that has ever been recorded was at the top of Mount Washington, in New Hampshire, (231 miles per hour).

The "prevailing wind" is a region where the wind is almost always blowing in one direction. Over much of Europe and North America, the wind is westerly; in the Caribbean, it is generally easterly. In some regions the wind does not blow in one general direction, but consists of little gusts and lulls. At a given temperature, the air is cooler if there is a wind and warmer if there is no wind. When the wind is strong it really gets cool—this effect is called the wind chill. Wind is usually measured with instruments known as anemometers.

When cattle lie down early in the morning, it will rain before night.

A simple cup anemometer is a set of three or four conical shaped vanes about the size of a tea cup mounted on arms which rotate on a vertical spindle. A counting device is used to indicate the number of revolutions in a given time interval, and from this number the wind speed can be obtained by referring to a table supplied with the instrument. Anemometers can also be attached to a constant-reading gauge.

Just as there are winds in the lower atmosphere, there are also winds higher up, and there is a considerable difference between them. Up to about 2,000 feet, the wind speed increases with altitude. We know, for instance, that if the air in the upper atmosphere is unstable, fast moving air from above moves quickly to the surface and creates a commotion on the ground. But if the upper atmosphere is stable, the fast moving air stays up in the heavens and the surface air is calm. From 2,000 feet upward, the winds increase in force as they near the troposphere and these are important to the pilots of modern aircraft who have to deal with headwinds of 100 mph or more when cruising the friendly skies. The most fascinating of these upper-air winds are the jet streams, high level cores of fast moving air that occur in temperate latitudes. Just imagine, if you will, the long skirt of a young lady as she swirls violently to the strain of a square dance. As she twirls, the hem of the skirt weaves like a roller coaster. Up and down the skirt goes. This absolutely silly example of the whirling skirt, I think, best describes the general movement of the jet stream as it makes its way across the various continents. During the winter of

1979, the jet stream was to our north, so the warm temperatures of the south kept us, here in the Northeast, quite warm and deliriously happy. (There were other reasons such as a high pressure system positioned over the Great Lakes that constantly kept pushing all the snow storms down south. Virginia, for example, was buried under tons of snow while we were brushing off the lawn chairs and cleaning our sunglasses.)

When we go way up, say 100,000 feet or higher, our knowledge is not as great, but we do know that at about 50 to 200 miles there are a group of ionized gases (electrified molecules). This is the area we previously mentioned as the ionosphere. These ions have the property of being able to reflect radio waves, bending them to the curved surface of the earth. Without this phenomenon there couldn't be loud, blaring radios on the streets and trains. Also found in the region from 30 to 50 miles up is a layer of ozone. Ozone is formed, thank goodness, from oxygen, by the action of the ultra violet light in the sun's rays. This layer effectively keeps these harmful rays from reaching the earth's surface. Without it, we would all become a collective flambe. In fact, life could not exist on earth.

When the down of a dandilion closes up, it is a sign of rain.

If a crow hollers

in the morning,

expect rain by night.

Which leads us to the concepts of radiation. Radiation consists of electromagnetic waves traveling at the speed of light, or 186,282 miles per second. Light from the sun, which is situated about 93 million miles away, arrives on the earth in eight minutes.

The energy of the sun is arriving continuously at a rate of 1.35 kilowatts per square meter when the sun is directly overhead. This figure is referred to as the solar constant. But less energy than this actually arrives on the surface. This is because of clouds, dust, and water vapor that absorbs some of the sun's energy as it passes through the atmosphere. If the air is clear, most of the radiation passes down to the surface and is absorbed or reflected. So you can see that the absorbed energy heats up the surface and the surface warms up the air

When rabbits seek shelter in the low lands, snow is on the way.

above like the old flame under a pot of water. Some of the radiation is trapped as it starts heading out again and so the atmosphere keeps the surface warmer than it otherwise would be. This is commonly known as the "greenhouse effect." Thus we know that radiation is received from the sun during the day but the temperature just doesn't continue going up all day long. It reaches a maximum temperature during mid-afternoon and then it decreases. So, when you look up at the sky somewhere around two or three o'clock in the afternoon and the sun is still pretty much overhead, you must realize that the temperature is beginning to decrease. This all occurs because the earth is constantly losing heat by radiation—the higher the temperature, the greater the loss. It's really quite remarkable to see that in the early afternoon the good earth's radiation begins to offset the sun's radiation and the cooling process starts. This entire process of diminishing returns continues until sunrise when the lowest temperature is finally achieved. Of course, if the sky is cloudy, then both the incoming and outgoing radiation is slowed up somewhat. I am sure you dread those clear winter nights when the process of radiational cooling sets in and we use up to $100 worth of fuel in one night.

When a squirrel eats nuts high in the tree
The weather will be as warm as warm can be.

When through the dismal night the lone wolf howls,
Or when at eve around the house he prowls,
And, grown familiar, seeks to make his bed,
Careless of man, in some outlying shed,
Then mark: ere thrice the sun shall arise,
A horrid storm will sweep the blackened sky.

Aratus

Seasons

To me, the changing of the seasons is nothing short of a miracle. The changing seasons, with their different lengths of day and night and the mad array of weather events, arise from the changing attitude of the earth's relationship to the sun. In fact, the earth has an axis to grind and so it continuously points in one direction in space, inclined at an angle of 66 ½ ° to the plane of the earth's orbit. In winter, when Exxon is holding us all up at gunpoint, the northern hemisphere, or better, the North Pole, is tilted away from the sun during the winter solstice (December 22); the sun does not shine at all on the Arctic Circle for a period of twenty-four hours, and we in the northern hemisphere have the shortest day in the year. In the summer, when Exxon is pretending to look for oil on the continental shelf, the summer solstice (June 21) occurs. This time the sun shines for 24 hours straight in the Arctic Circle and we in the northern hemisphere have the longest day in the year. As you can imagine, the entire process is quite the reverse in the southern hemisphere. By the way, the sun is higher in the sky in the summer than in the winter as a result of the changing inclination of the earth relative to the sun. The actual difference between the sun's position in the heavens during midsummer and midwinter is about 47°. This explains why the solar rays strike the earth at a more direct angle in the summer and produce a greater heating effect.

We have already mentioned that the oceans respond less significantly to the seasons' changes and that they are cooler in the summer and warmer in the winter. Surfaces that are covered with snow reflect away a large part of the solar radiation and this is easily noticeable when you are shown slides of the polar regions and wonder why such sunny skies don't melt the permanent snow cover. Incidentally, the sun's direct rays return to the northern hemisphere during spring when the vernal equinox takes place and the days start to get a little longer.

I love the New England seasons, and although we may squawk at a particularly miserable winter storm and wish we could transport ourselves to Arizona or Florida for life, remember that a New Englander would rather suffer and enjoy the slight changes that signal a new season: a crocus, those tulips, the forsythia, the running of sap in the maples, and the return of the robin is eminently more exciting than looking at a tree that you know will have its leaves glued on for at least a century.

Lions become nervous when a storm approaches.

Water and Clouds

Let's talk a little about water. At a Hollywood restaurant, W.C. Fields was once asked if he would like a glass of water. He responded by intoning, "Never touch the stuff, fish make love in it." He chose another word, but what the heck. Water, water everywhere and most of it is evaporating at a rate equal to the way the I.R.S. vaporizes our paychecks. Water evaporates from the ground, the oceans, from puddles, from lakes and rivers, and even the sweat of your brow. Water vapor is constantly being formed. Just drive into any outdoor movie and you won't be able to see a thing through the windshields of a thousand cars. In fact, water vapor stays in the air as long as it stays warm.

Red sky at morning, sailors take warning;
Red sky at night, sailor's delight.

Those molecules we talked about earlier keep bouncing about very quickly and only when the situation becomes cooler do the molecules decide they should stick together. When this happens, we see the result as a liquid. But evaporation also occurs through roots or large areas of vegetation by a process known as transpiration. This evaporated water is lifted up to the sky and carried by the winds until it permeates the entire troposphere; in fact, the wind carries the vapors to the interior land masses. The air becomes cooled by various processes and according to the altitude and temperature, will form a cloud, rain, fog, and anything else of a precipitative nature. Of course, most of the water is returned to the earth in the form of snow or rain, so there is a relentless process of exchange of water between the land, sea, and atmosphere. This is called the water cycle. Every ten days the water cycle is completed and the process repeats itself

If the bull leads the cows to pasture, rain is coming.

once again. There are times when water vapor is carried high up in the celestial dome, and when it cools, it condenses on grains of dust in the same manner as fog, only fog in the sky is known as a cloud. Actually, at those altitudes, they are really ice crystals around water droplets that are called condensation nuclei.

Remember when we spoke of how the temperature decreases with height? We said about a 20 °F drop is possible at an altitude of 5,000 feet. In the formation of a cloud, this process of cooling is revealed by decompression or expansion, which is the result of the upward movement of warm air. When this occurs in an unstable atmosphere, and depending on the mood of the air mass and its temperature and humidity, condensation begins and this level marks the base of the cloud. The top of the cloud, which can look like an atomic explosion, is the level at which the air is stable. This process is known as convection and the cloud formed as a result of its intervention is called a cumulus cloud. You see them all the time as those cotton balls gleaming like so many golf balls against an azure sky. Sometimes when the atmosphere is turbulent, the vertical movement of air is pushed about by the wind and the clouds do not appear like so many golf balls but rather like small filaments huddled together.

So instead of those separate entities in the sky, we perceive a continuous layer of clouds that look like a gigantic bedsheet across the heavens. Thus it would behoove us to create a classification of clouds.

Clouds come in all sizes and occur at all levels of the troposphere, but for our purposes we will divide them into three classes according to altitude. But before we begin our survey, I must add that it was the Frenchman, LaMark, a naturalist, who first suggested the system of classifying clouds in 1802. It was another gentleman by the name of Luke Howard, from England, who insisted on using Latin names to describe the various cloud formations. The popularity of the Latin usage has allowed it to endure to the present.

Low clouds found at 6,500 feet or under:
Stratus (St): A grey layer of cloud that resembles fog but does not rest on the ground. It comes from the Latin "to extend."
Nimbostratus (NbSt): A low dark layer of cloud which sprinkles us with rain or snow. From the Latin "rainy cloud."
Cumulus (Cu): These are those brilliant white clouds against the blue sky that are flat at the base and look like cauliflower at the tops. They are fair weather clouds unless they are very large, in which case they could produce rain. From the Latin "to heap or pile."
Cumulonimbus (CuNb): This is the spectacular one they call the thundercloud and it can rise up to an altitude of 50,000 feet. It looks

When dogs rub themselves in winter, it will thaw soon.

When rooks fly high, the next day will be fair.

like a mountain although it resembles the top of a cumulus cloud. This one produces heavy rains with thunder and lightning.

Stratocumulus (StCu): A layer of clouds that appear like flat cumulus and are grey in color.

Now let us venture to the middle clouds and see if you can recognize any of the descriptions. These clouds appear at an altitude of 6,500 feet to 20,000 feet. This is why they use the prefix alto before the same names we used to describe the low clouds:

Altostratus (ASt): I am sure you have seen this grey layer of cloud that seems to extend forever in all directions. It is a depressing cloud that allows the sun to shine only partially and then thickens and lowers, becoming nimbostratus which, of course, produces rain.

Altocumulus (ACu): Most often this formation resembles a round saucer that is grey in the middle and white on the outside. They are arranged in a regular manner as in groups of lines. Sometimes you can see the blue sky between them, or they may fuse together and look like a honeycomb.

Well, we have arrived at the top and the high clouds described here are called cirrus from the Latin "a lock of hair" or "a bird's tuft." These clouds are usually white and thin or feathery in appearance and occur at a height of 20,000 to 50,000 feet. I am dizzy already:

Cirrus (Ci): These are the aristocratic clouds that resemble delicate feathers and are popularly called "mare's tails." They do not block out the sun and are composed mainly of ice crystals.

Cirrostratus (CiSt): This is the white sheet of cloud that gives the sky a milky appearance. It can also produce a halo around the sun or moon. It's deceptive and can become a nimbostratus and is regarded as a sign of rain.

Cirrocumulus (CiCu): Many consider this the prettiest formation of them all. These are small luscious white cloudlets arranged in lines, groups, or ripples, that have been given the name of "mackeral sky."

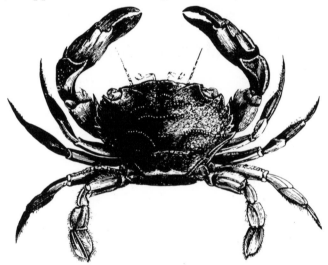

Before the storm the crab his briny home
sidelong forsakes, and strives on land to roam.

I guess the only way these descriptions of clouds are going to make any sense at all is to perhaps look at them in the manner of their appearance. Okay. So right now the sky is clear, but you go out early tomorrow morning, some changes have occurred, and you want to make some sense of the sky's latest attire. We earlier spoke of air masses and mentioned how, in the northern hemisphere, they are constantly moving from west to east, and how these can settle in your area after traveling the entire country. For example, we could be in a stuck tropical air mass and suffer the broiling effects of a scorching sun and hot breeze. Relief can come about as the result of the intervention of a polar air mass sweeping down from Canada, finally ending this horrendous sauna. These air masses always bring with them their own particular gifts and sometimes we don't want any part of their generosity. The actual weather you receive, though, doesn't necessarily depend on the kind of air mass that visits your region. It also has to depend on the kind of land that receives it. For example, hot land may take that tropical mass and create thunder showers that quickly result in a clearing trend. Cold land may receive the same air mass and turn it into fog.

When an owl hoots, rain is coming.

117

If a cat's fur looks glossy, it will be pleasant the next day.

Frontology

The boundary between two different air masses is called a "front." It is obvious that no one in his/her right mind would call a "front" a "back" because a front is where all the action is in terms of rain and thunder, and a "back" is not worth mentioning at all. And although an air mass may contain conditions that are uniform throughout, quite sharp changes occur in the smaller area of the front. As a front passes a given area, important changes happen to the temperature, wind direction, and the clouds.

The most important fronts are those that have big differences: warm, damp air on one side and cold dry air on the other. Backs are limited in their scope of intellectual pursuits and so they are only given certificates in "backing," a form of wind change where the winds shift counterclockwise, from northeast to northwest, for example.

Now wait a minute. What does a counterclockwise movement of air have to do with fronts? Plenty. A front, in order to be well dressed for the occasion, must have a "low" attached to it in order to have a degree of efficacy. You see, a "low," or cyclone as it is called in exalted circles, is the cousin of the high of which we will speak of in due course. Here air pressure is sort of low at the center and increases toward the outside of the low. The wind circulation about the center

The goose and the gander'
Begin to meander;
The matter is plain,
They are dancing for rain.

is counterclockwise or cyclonic (as they say in imperious circles) where the strongest winds are often found at the center. So what does this have to do with the price of gas at the pump? Plenty. This low has a strong upward motion at its center and the result usually is cloudy weather, often producing lots of precipitation. In contrast to highs, lows do not have uniform characteristics over their widths—these things are 500 to 1,000 miles across. Instead, the darlings are marked

When rain is coming, horses' tails appear larger.

119

by boundaries called "fronts" where the wind, pressure, humidity, temperature, and cloud features dramatically change for the better (or worse).

There are only four fronts to speak of: cold, warm, stationary, and occluded. At the forefront of these little trouble makers is the cold front. In a cold front (get this) a warm air mass is followed by a cold air mass. If the cold air is retreating so that as the front passes over a place, the temperature there goes up, the front is called a warm front. Isn't this a painful lesson in frontology? Along the warm front, the warm air is rising in a sloping manner and is therefore subject to cooling and condensation. About 500 miles ahead of the front you will notice some cirrus clouds and as the front advances, the clouds gradually lower and thicken (nimbostratus) and we get some rain. The heaviest rains occur where the trailing portion of the front passes by at ground level. When the front passes by, the temperature starts to go up and the clouds break up. When a cold front passes by, it pro-

Deer and elk come down from the mountains at least two days before a bad storm.

When rats and mice move shavings away from the windward side of the house, it is going to storm.

duces a similar event but in reverse, but the change is more violent because of the greater slope created. Imagine cold air pushing that warm air straight up into the troposphere creating those ominous thunderclouds we mentioned earlier.

Sometimes a front refuses to budge and it is called a stationary front. On the other hand one front may move so quickly that it overtakes another. When this happens, the temperature difference across this occluded front marks the boundary between the air ahead of the slower front and the air behind the faster front. Fascinating stuff.

Now highs don't need fronts attached to their coat tails because they are happy and quite peaceful. When there is a veering trend to the air, the flow changes or shifts to a clockwise flow, say northeast to southeast. This flow is called anticyclonic. A high pressure area is usually several hundred miles in diameter and has high pressure at its center and somewhat lower pressure at its edges. This pressure distribution causes the air to travel in the clockwise or anticyclonic manner. The wind is generally light at the center and stronger at the edges. The air not only moves in a circle but also moves downward at the center. This of course is what creates the clear skies associated with a high pressure area.

Each night as you tune in on your favorite news show, a rather funny fellow appears on the screen toward the end of the program (as I mentioned earlier he is purposely put there so that you have to watch the entire show before you can get the weather. Those new

When starlings swarm in large numbers, expect rain.

directors are devilish fellows and know that a good weather person can hold the ratings at a level pace). As the camera zooms in on the massive studio map of the United States, you are immediately confused by all the funny symbols hanging magically over the Great Lakes. You also notice a rather long, linguine-type line that has triangles or semi-circles attached to it. The credible yet endearing weatherman or lady then explains, in two minutes or less (I usually get about 20 seconds to do my thing), what the weather is and what it will become. For example, "A ridge of high pressure in eastern Canada held those clouds at bay over the Great Lakes and we had a cool but great day here in Wheeling, West Virginia. But all things must change—a warm front is advancing from the west and the skies are going to cloud up by early tomorrow." By this time the camera man is usually giving the weatherman a wrap-up signal, and the rest of the explanation is left up to you to figure out. This is probably why lots of you are confused about how a front works and what to look for before a storm.

Let's say the weatherman had an understanding boss who allowed him to report the weather to its logical conclusion. The report would then continue on thusly, "Well, the front is really far away and some 500 miles ahead of it (and about five miles high) the sky is already giving you a signal about what is to come. Those high cirrus clouds are already here. Look up and you will see feather-like clouds with lots of blue sky around them. Well, they are the beginning of a series of steps that we could refer to as the battle of the air. Simply put, the warm air is advancing and the cool air is retreating, so the area where the warm front arrives has a rise in temperature. That is why they call it a warm front. Warm air is lighter than cold air and rises over the cold air forming a sloping situation where the cold air is pushed downward and backwards. The first thing you notice are the cirrus clouds, about eight miles up, and in about twelve hours when you look again, the clouds will take on another appearance. They will be thin, milky, and flat as a pancake. They have in fact lowered and thickened; the advancing air has changed them from harmless cirrus to cirrostratus (milky) to altostratus (that depressing grey cloud that goes on forever) and finally to nimbostratus (a low dark layer of clouds). The rain belt is actually 200 miles ahead of the front and the heaviest rain will occur when the trailing portion passes at ground level. After the front has passed, the temperature will begin to rise, the rain will end, and the clouds begin to break up.'' Now wouldn't you like to hear that sometime on a weather show. I doubt very much if you ever will.

A cold front advances in exactly the same manner, except in reverse. The change will probably be more violent and rapid because the slope that we described in the warm front is greater. It's a warm

When a turkey stands with his back to the wind, a storm is coming

123

day in Hanover, New Hampshire, and a cold front is approaching. This cold front is about 700 miles wide and goes straight up over ten miles. We are now in the forward moving area and an advancing polar air mass is trying to push back some tropical air and the first thing you notice is some light fog or some haze which is what happens when the warm air is chilled near the ground. Then, a wild bunch of inconsiderate and menacing thunderclouds (the ones that resemble the grey mountain) start to deliver a drenching rain shower that strikes the earth like a bunch of arrows. The reason for this madness can be explained as a mass of cold air lifting the warm moist air high into the heavens with great force; the winds whirl and blow at great speeds because of the violent circulation of the cold and hot air. But just as quickly as it arrives, the old son of a gun is gone. First it's warm and then it's stormy and then it's cool. The cloud formations are often the exact reverse of a warm front, starting with cumulonimbus, then altostratus, cirrostratus, and those lovely cirrus clouds return and the sky quickly clears out. Fronts are a vivacious lot and bring with them all sorts of changes.

If goats leave their home during a rain, it will soon clear.

When cocks crow and then drink,
Rain and thunder are on the brink.

Rain, Snow, Hail, and Other Things

The rain in Spain stays mainly on the plain. How does it rain? Well, the cloud story certainly afforded us the opportunity to study how clouds look and in what order they appear before and after a front. But let's start with the littlest rain, that rain we call "drizzle." Drizzle is that fine mist that slowly destroys a hairdo from the time it takes to walk from the parking lot to the Grange Hall. One doesn't use an umbrella during a drizzle because it somehow seems cowardly. Drizzle is a sort of mist and is composed of small liquid droplets that are less than two hundredths of an inch (0.02) in diameter, and they usually fall from stratus clouds. Anything larger than 0.02 inches is considered rain and for all the math majors who have read this far, raindrops vary in diameter from 1/2 to 5½ millimeters. When the big ones fall, air resistance establishes a maximum falling speed of about 8 meters (25 feet) per second.

Most cloud droplets are constantly floating in space and a process has to occur that can change them to raindrop size. Just imagine a cloud formed in air at a temperature at just about freezing. Many of these droplets do not freeze but rather remain in a supercooled state.

Or to put it another way, some of the droplets *do* freeze, and it takes both the frozen and the supercooled drops to tango in order for the tangible results to appear on our streets. If we have a cloud temperature of − 40 °F, a temperature where even the stoutest heart is no longer allowed to love, we find that all water droplets freeze. But usually we have a cloud that contains both ice particles and water droplets. Now comes the best part because the relative humidity of the air that is in contact with the water droplets differs from that in contact with the ice; for the water droplets, the humidity is just below the saturation point and for the ice just above the saturation point. The water droplets will evaporate, but the vapor will condense on the ice particles. The ice particles win the contest and keep growing, to

When swans fly against the wind, rain is coming.

the bewilderment or expense of the water droplets. As the ice particles grow in size and weight, they fall into warmer air and melt into raindrops. I guess you could say that ice particles have to become obese by consuming lots of vapor before taking the big plunge.

In places like Tahiti, where the clouds don't contain ice, there is another process that transpires in the great rain story, a process called coalescence. Here the rain drops don't have much competition from ice particles, so some large drops falling through the slower falling small drops grab them in mid-air and hold them prisoner while growing larger every foot of the way. Larger drops are then formed and the rain falls in joyous streams.

If you want to measure rain, don't bring out a ruler and stick it on the front lawn because you may become the laughing stock of the town. Rainfall is usually expressed in millimeters, but you could use good old inches if you want. If 5 mm of rain falls on a particular day, it is considered rainy. One inch of rain (25 mm) is undoubtedly a *very* wet day. In order to measure the rain, a simple rain gauge can be fashioned by using a plastic funnel in a bottle that is itself protected from the rain. The water collected in the bottle is then poured into a rain gauge that has graduations so designed that the amount of rainfall can be read easily. The heaviest rains fall out of cloudbursts that last only a few minutes and can fill up a given drainage system and cause flooding. If it doesn't rain for a long time, the result is a

Rams leap about and butt each other before a storm.

drought. A partial drought occurs when over a period of 29 days less than 0.01 inches fall over a given area.

Despite the protestations of many of us, a dry quiet snow can be beautiful and at times can bring equilibrium out of the chaos of daily struggle. There is peace in watching the eternal mantle of white covering up otherwise empty tree limbs, and in a sense it is a sort of spring without the flowers. We spoke earlier of the water-ice transfer and how this creates rain. But here we see that the ice crystals mass together and form snowflakes. The water vapor in the clouds is cooled so much that instead of forming raindrops, it freezes into snowflakes.

Hares go to the woods before a severe storm.

By the way, snow is not formed like hail or sleet. Snow is formed directly out of the water vapor in the clouds while sleet or hail are born from large clusters of water vapor which first were raindrops and then froze up. You have probably seen those large wet snowflakes that hit the ground and then disappear as if by magic on the pavement. Well, snow can fall to the ground at a temperature as high as 39 °F. But if it is very cold, snow falls like a dry powder and this powdery snow is not too slippery on the roads. But we here in the Northeast have to contend with snow that approaches the melting point so often, that the ballet of the cars continues for a good part of the winter. Ten inches of fresh snow is the equivalent to about one inch of rain.

A thunderstorm is a wild happening filled with lightning, thunder, heavy rain, and wild winds. You can tell when a thunderstorm is in the vicinity because a thundercloud (cumulonimbus) with a flat base and a top that looks like an anvil will hover menacingly over everything. This cloud can rise to an altitude of thirty thousand feet or more and the wind that comes before it appears as a gust as you stand toward the cloud. Then the wind dies down and a gust hits you from another direction and the rain finally falls quickly. The pyrotechnics arise as the result of electrical charges. Inside the cloud a great turbulence has dispersed the raindrops and the smaller droplets are carried to the top of the cloud while the larger ones remain at the lowest level. This entire process of separation leads inevitably to a separation of electrical charges. When the insulation of the air is broken, a flash of lightning becomes evident either within the cloud itself or as a spectacular vision in the sky. The tops of the clouds have the positive charges and the lower parts have the negative charges.

Hail can also fall from thunderstorms and can be quite large. A raindrop near the bottom of the cloud becomes caught in an updraft and is carried toward the colder realms. Here it freezes and gathers ice crystals in the upper cloud and becomes larger and falls. In the lower part of the cloud there is more water to be collected and then another updraft may send it scurrying up again to the top, freezing it again. In fact, hail can take on monstrous proportions, sometimes even approaching the size of a baseball. Needless to say, if you're ever caught in a hail storm, get thee under cover.

How can anyone forget an ice storm in New England. Ice can be extremely dangerous and is formed as rain falls from only a few hundred feet from the ground where there is warm air. When the drops become supercooled (drops that do not freeze but remain liquid), they hit the surface and freeze immediately causing skidding conditions. This is the sort of ice that creates the haunting beauty of iced limbs and wires and sends photographers scrambling all over the place.

Bears are always restless before a storm.

So there we have what I call "A Kind of a Short Course in Weather." It's obvious that meteorology is a complex and demanding science, and I, for one, find it fascinating and confusing. If I've confused you along the way, I apologize, but only hope that I have whetted your interest enough to make you go out and learn more about this subject — there are plenty of good books (and more serious ones than this) available.

In fact, you might even want to build your own weather station. All you'll need is a rain gauge, an anemometer, a wind vane, a compass, a barometer, and a wet and dry bulb hygrometer. With all these formidable materials, you would then have the means to forcast your own weather on a daily basis with a degree of accuracy equivalent to the big boys at the real weather station. But this could run you into the hundreds of dollars, and I would think it best to use your Yankee ingenuity and find materials in your own home to construct a home weather station. This will cost you nothing, in fact, except perhaps a couple of weekends of work in the privacy of your garage or basement. This is always a good way to instruct your children on the elementary study of meteorology, and besides, that guy on television is wrong sometimes, and you can phone him up on days when you are more accurate than he is. Remember the family that makes weather stations together stays together.

I found a fascinating little book by Herman Schneider called *Everyday Weather* in which Mr. Schneider skillfully and entertainingly details in plain language the construction of a weather station for young people using everyday materials found around the house. I will go a step further and say that not only can younger people derive pleasure from this undertaking but older people can also. I know because I fashioned a Schneider Weather Station and it works quite well indeed. So shut the television off and get your rusty hammer ready and some glue and courage, and perhaps the weather will never be a mystery to you again. The name of the book is *Everyday Weather and How It Works* by Herman Schneider, New York, McGraw-Hill Book Company, 1961. Get it — it's great!

Glossary

Glossary

Air: The stuff we breathe. A mixture of gases composed mainly of nitrogen and oxygen. When a politician is present, the air is usually hot.

Air Mass: A big hunk of air whose temperature and moisture content is usually uniform. In the summer we love those polar air masses, while in the winter, the tropical ones are favored.

Anemometer: An instrument that usually looks like two stiff training bras whirling around that measures the velocity of the wind.

Anticyclone: While this sounds like the name of a radical group opposed to storms, it is really a system characterized by high pressure with winds blowing clockwise.

Backing: When the winds shift to counterclockwise.

Barometric Pressure: The weight of the atmosphere on a specific unit area above a given point. Generally, the lower the pressure, the wilder it gets.

Climate: The long-term state of the weather at a place or over an area usually expressed as a result of temperature and precipitation. Arizona, for example, has a different climate than Chicago. (And New York has a different climate than Tierra del Fuego.)

Coastal System: What we in New England call a ''nor'easter.'' A cyclonic system moving along the coast causing north to east winds and usually stormy.

Cold Front: The transition zone between advancing cold air and retreating warm air. Also the attitude taken by a reluctant female.

Condensation: The opposite of evaporation. When a substance changes from vapor form to solid form.

Convection: The transfer of heat in the air, particularly in the vertical drafts of a thermal, the things that gliders thrive on.

Cyclone: Obviously, the opposite of an anticyclone. A system characterized by low pressure with winds blowing counterclockwise.

Depression: An area of low pressure (which can be *very* depressing to people in the Caribbean when they hear of the development of a "tropical depression"—the forerunner of a hurricane).

Dew: Water droplets formed by condensation of water vapor, usually caused by overnight cooling. Particularly pretty on spider webs.

Dew Point: The temperature at which air reaches saturation as it cools. An important measure in New York in the summer (tells you approximately how awful it's going to be).

Evaporation: When a substance changes from the liquid stage to the gaseous or vapor stage. The opposite of condensation.

Filling: An increase of pressure at the center of a storm system.

Front: The transition zone between two air masses having different characteristics, say warm air and cold air. Fronts are responsible for most of our weather changes.

Frontology: No such word; a Tiradoism used in this book to try to explain fronts.

Frost: Ice crystals formed by sublimation of water vapor in the air; usually attributed to a fellow named Jack.

Gale: Winds with speeds from 38-55 miles per hour. Not a good time to go sailing.

Gust: A brief, temporary increase in the speed of the wind. Those puffs of air that send papers and skirts flying.

High: Not what you think it is. This time it means a pressure system with high pressure at the center. Usually associated with fair, cool weather.

Humidity: A measure of the amount of water vapor in the air. High humidity is what makes us feel so lazy and inept in the summer.

Hurricane: A storm characterized by extremely low barometric pressure and winds in excess of 74 miles per hour; usually very destructive; usually have silly names.

Instability: A mental feeling generated by trying to write a glossary. In meteorology, though, it means a situation in the atmosphere where air will tend to continue to rise and move farther from its original level.

Jet Stream: A ''river'' of fast moving air in the upper atmosphere, usually moving from west to east and having broad effects on our weather. Also, a famous race horse.

Land Breeze: A light breeze blowing from the land towards the sea, usually during the night when the land is cooler than the sea.

Low: A pressure system with low pressure at the center, usually associated with less than perfect weather.

Mackeral Sky: Popular name for the pretty cirrocumulus clouds.

Mare's Tails: The popular name for the elegant, high-altitude cirrus clouds; composed mainly of ice crystals.

Mean Temperature: No, not a nasty temperature, but the average temperature at a given place over a period of time. The mean daily temperature is usually the average of the minimum and maximum temperatures for a 24-hour period.

Mist: This is that very light fog condition, where things are damp but the visibility is not too restricted.

Nor'easter: A New England coastal storm featuring gale force winds from the north and east.

Occluded Front: A combination of two fronts produced when a cold front overtakes a warm front, forcing the warm air to rise.

Ozone Layer: A layer in the upper atmosphere (30 to 50 miles up) composed of a relatively high amount of ozone. This layer helps to filter the sun's ultra violet rays, and make life liveable on earth.

Polar Air: An air mass formed over northern Canada and most welcome in New York in August (but not in January). It is somewhat warmer and wetter than an arctic air mass.

Precipitation: This is the stuff that falls out of the sky: rain, snow, sleet, hail, drizzle, cats, dogs, etc.

Relative Humidity: The ratio of the amount of water vapor in the air to the amount that could be present if the air at the same temperature were saturated. It is usually expressed as a percentage, and you know it when it's high.

Saturation: When a hunk of air holds the maximum amount of water vapor (when the relative humidity is 100%).

Sea Breeze: A light wind which blows from the sea to the land, usually during daylight hours when the land is warmer than the sea. This is why coastal areas are often much cooler than inland areas during the summer.

Semi-Permanent High or Low: These are the fairly stationary and stable pressure systems such as the Bermuda High or the Icelandic Low.

Squall: A sudden, strong wind lasting only a short while. Squalls, to be reported, must have winds in excess of 18 miles per hour and last for 2 minutes or more. Otherwise, it would qualify only as a gust.

Squall Line: A line of serious instability preceding a cold front and characterized by strong winds, turbulence, and heavy showers; usually of short duration.

Stationary Front: A front that gets stuck, that does not show signs of movement over a period of time.